ICEBREAKERS

ICEBREAKERS

A Sourcebook of Games, Exercises and Simulations

KEN JONES

Kogan Page, London

First published in Great Britain in 1991
by Kogan Page Ltd
120 Pentonville Road, London N1 9JN

Reprinted in 1992 (twice)

Designed, arranged and typeset by Ken Jones using an Archimedes computer together with the desktop publishing package Impression and a LaserDirect printer, both by Computer Concepts Ltd

Printed and bound in Great Britain by
Biddles Ltd, Guildford and King's Lynn

British Library Cataloguing in Publication Data

A CIP record for this book is available from the British Library

ISBN (UK) 0 7494 0803 0

SMARAN WEBB

Contents

Acknowledgements

Authors of icebreakers need guinea pigs. So my grateful thanks are due to the many people - administrators, bankers, business executives, police officers, psychologists, students, teachers, trainers - who participated.

As I invented the icebreakers, rather than collecting them, they have the imprint of my own particular way of thinking. Two events, however, incorporate the inspirations of others.

One is NEW NAMES in which players invent a secret name for themselves. The basic idea arose out of a conversation I had with Garry Shirts (author of the well-known activity STARPOWER) when I visited him in California. He described in fascinating detail an event in which the facilitator wrote a secret sign on the palm of each player's right hand. Points were scored for signs discovered, and points lost if more than one player knew one's own sign.

The other inspirational thought I adopted wholesale from David Crookall of the University of Alabama, who is editor of *Simulation and Gaming*. He inspected the manuscript of this book and was amused by some of the initials - for example, the National Archaeological and Sociological Association in MONOLITH. He suggested that in MAGICIANS I should change the Noble Guild of Magicians to the Magnificent Guild of Magicians. It is a pleasure to incorporate this hidden tribute to Hollywood.

1

Ice, and what to do about it

The metaphor of icebreaking is apt. An icebreaker is a vessel designed to clear a passage in frozen waters and open up channels of communication. In human terms icebreakers are intended to deal with frosty situations, cold starts, nervous freezing. They aim not only to break ice but also to warm the atmosphere. A 'warm-up' is another is name for an icebreaker. By contrast the social mixing and introductions in everyday life are very hit and miss. They can be difficult: one can forget names, not know what to say, and if embarrassment turns into panic then the mind can go completely blank or one can burble like an idiot. An icebreaker helps to overcome such problems.

Icebreakers are not limited to activities at the beginning of courses. They can be used whenever ice has frozen communication. If, halfway through a course (conference, convention, workshop), the trainees (students, conference-goers) have formed themselves into cliques based on sex or race or jobs, or any other criteria, then an icebreaker could be well worth while.

Another important consideration is that icebreakers can do other things as well. For example, they can develop skills, create talking points, illustrate situations in the real world. Thus, they could be used irrespective of their icebreaking properties if they meet the needs of a course or session. The label 'icebreaker' should not deter trainers and teachers from using the events in other situations where they would be effective.

The icebreakers in this book are all interactive, all designed to help people to mix in a variety of situations. If ice has formed because of a work situation ('Couldn't you see I was busy?', 'You should not have shouted at me') then an icebreaker can be useful for its facility to conjure up a situation not pre-loaded with tension, dislike and mutual misunderstanding.

I invented the icebreakers in this book with the above aims in mind. In contrast to many other icebreakers, I tried to avoid the trivial and the childish. I left out party games. There is no fanning a balloon across a chalk line, no catching a plate before it stops spinning.

Nor are there any psycho-therapeutic events. Participants are not asked to reveal their innermost feelings. Missing are all those activities where a person stands in the middle of a group and falls only to be pushed upright again by supportive members. Also missing are the dramatic roleplays in which people have to playact - something which many find difficult and some may regard as an invasion of their privacy. Such events can be icemakers rather than icebreakers. So in this book no one has to pretend to be a father with a daughter who has a drugs problem, or to playact someone suffering from AIDS. This book does not treat the participants as patients, or actors, or children. This is not because there is anything wrong with party games, psychotherapy, or drama sessions. They are all very useful and respectable techniques. The reason that none are included here is that the aim is to break ice, not have personality probes, playacting performances, or sessions of juvenile fun.

Several books containing icebreakers and other interactive events give the impression that icebreakers are short, trivial and not worthy of much consideration. Some books contain hundreds of such events, each restricted to a skimpy page of general notes which suggests that quantity is preferable to quality.

Most 'serious' icebreakers tend to be dull, offering little challenge to the intellect or the imagination. Usually they are perfunctory exercises of the 'getting to know you' type, where the participants move around for 20 minutes and ask each other about their hobbies. This can give the impression that the participants are being treated like children - in contrast to the adult demands made on them in the course itself.

Of course, some icebreakers are brilliant and imaginative, but these are extremely rare. What often happens is that the chosen icebreakers are so inappropriate that they create their own ice and the facilitator can be faced with polite but frosty resistance.

The icebreakers in this book attempt to challenge the participants in a variety of ways - intellectual, imaginative, artistic, diplomatic, managerial, organizational - all involving communication skills. All have notes for the facilitator and the participants. Most include documents for the participants: this in itself is a signal that the facilitator is treating the activity (and the participants) with respect. I have tried to provide plenty of scope for mind jogging, for humour, for amusing initiatives. I hope this book will provoke events that can be appreciated and enjoyed on an adult level. Enjoyment, when meeting people, is an excellent way of breaking ice.

Three categories - games, exercises, simulations

This book is probably unique in its field by distinguishing between games, exercises and simulations based on the thoughts and behaviour of the participants. What matters is not the label on the outside of the package, nor the worthy aims of the author or facilitator. Events are not books, and are not aims. The key question in any interactive learning event is - how many participants are treating the activity:

(a) as a game in which players have a duty to try to win
(b) as an exercise dealing with problems, puzzles, issues
(c) as a simulation involving 'professional' roles and functions?

Most books use 'game', 'simulation' and 'exercise' interchangeably, with results ranging from mild dissatisfaction to active resentment, hurt, and ill feelings. Some participants may assume the event is a game, others treat it as an intellectual problem to be solved, while others accept professional real-world commitment and become annoyed with those who do not.

The facilitators become victims by unwittingly passing on the interchangeable labels to their students and nobody is in a position to discover what really went wrong since they lack the diagnostic tools for doing so. The facilitator blames the participants and the participants blame each other. Many authors add to the confusion by using 'actor' as interchangeable with 'player' which is like saying 'X is a good football actor' or 'Y acts good chess'. Here is an example (Liebrand 1983) of a piece of academic research into what Liebrand keeps referring to as 'social dilemma games':

> One of the most significant aspects of this study, however, did not show up in the data analysis. It is the extreme seriousness with which the subjects take the problems. Comments such as 'If you defect on the rest of us, you're going to live with it for the rest of your life' were not at all uncommon. Nor was it unusual for people to wish to leave the experimental building by the back door, to claim that they did not wish to see the 'sons of bitches' who double-crossed them, to become extremely angry at other subjects, or to become tearful.

Liebrand comments 'It is a common observation that in such instances subjects do take the decision task extremely seriously'. It is indeed a common observation. And two recurring features are the interchangeable terminology and the inability of the authors to offer any plausible explanation for what went wrong.

Academics tend to regard these sort of events as intellectual exercises, yet persist in calling them games, and are surprised at the emotion which is generated. The participants, on the other hand, are usually divided. Some treat it as a simulation and take on a professional role with real-world responsibilities and obligations. In the Liebrand example ('Prisoner's Dilemma') it is the role of criminals, hence the use of the term 'double-cross', which was presumably referring to 'honour among thieves'. The 'sons of bitches', on the other hand, undoubtedly thought they were in a game or an exercise. As gamesters they would assume that there were no real-world ethics involved and would see nothing dishonourable in taking advantage of the other 'players', provided they abided by the rules. The exercise people probably treated it as a puzzle of an intellectual type and they too would see nothing dishonourable about solving it to their own advantage, albeit to the disadvantage of their fellow 'problem-solvers'.

Both players and problem-solvers were probably shocked, hurt and resentful when they were accused of treachery, and one can assume that it was some of the gamesters and the problem-solvers who were reduced to tears following angry accusations by the participants who thought they were in a simulation. It is highly unlikely that anybody mentioned the possibility of incompatible methodologies, otherwise Liebrand (and other authors recounting similar situations) would have said so. The term I have coined for such events is 'ambivalents' (see Jones 1988) and experience suggests that ambivalents comprise a very large category indeed.

Some authors have argued that 'since everybody uses the labels interchangeably' the usage does not matter and that to look at the meanings is just a dry semantic debate about definitions. Maybe. But definitions do not become tearful and call each other 'sons of bitches'. Icebreakers are about people: people can get hurt and they matter. Facilitators are often so conscious of their aims and objectives that they overlook what is happening to the people in the events themselves.

In this book the categorizing of events by methodology is an attempt to minimize or avoid unnecessary unpleasantness, inefficiency and muddle.

Another protection against a methodological virus creeping into an event is a page entitled 'What are we supposed to do and why?' This can be photocopied and handed out on appropriate occasions. Obviously, the mental habits associated with the word 'game' are extremely resistant to a rethinking about what is really going on, but at least the page will provide tools for analysing the situation afterwards. It should prevent mistaking a clash of methods for a clash of personalities.

As argued above, the basic difference between the methodologies lies not in the materials but in the thoughts and behaviour of the participants. But there are differences in well-designed events which show up in the materials themselves and the procedure for running the events.

For example, in a game, Players' Notes embody the rules and are not out of place when the game is being played. Similarly, Participants' Notes in an exercise are part of the instructions and there is no reason why they should not be kept on the working surfaces. However, in simulations, Participants' Notes are incongruous in the boardroom or the market place or the hostile planet. They are for the briefing only, and should be removed before the action starts. Similarly, in games and exercises it does not matter too much if the activity takes place among the litter of everyday life - the piles of personal possessions, the company reports, the chemistry homework. But in most simulations this paraphernalia would be inappropriate as it contradicts the simulated environment and the professional roles. It detracts from the 'realism' of the event.

Other practical differences between the three categories can be seen by comparing the materials and procedures for the events contained in this book.

How to choose the icebreakers

The first and obvious way of choosing is by category. If you want competitive gaming behaviour then you need look no further than the chapter on games. If you want more co-operative behaviour centred on puzzles and problems rather than on winning then the chapter on exercises is the best starting place. If you want the participants to assume 'professional'-type roles, then the only section you need look at is the chapter on simulations.

It could, however, be a good idea to look at other ways of choosing to see whether these might be better suited to your needs.

The main alternative to choosing by category is to choose by subject matter: the summary of games, exercises and simulations in the next chapter is a handy reference for making comparisons and choices. Thus, if the course concerns business studies the obvious option is to pick events which involve managerial decision-making.

The exact opposite criteria to the above is to choose events which have nothing whatsoever to do with the subject matter of the course. The argument for doing this is that the event is an icebreaker and should have elements of the unusual, the amusing, the mind-jogging challenges. Some facilitators take the view that icebreakers are always better if they are different from the course itself and that if an event is chosen because of specific subjects then it should not be an icebreaker but an integral part of the course in its own right. If this is the argument then there are two separate criteria: (a) to pick an icebreaker which is unusual, innovative, mind-jogging, etc., and (b) to examine the events to see which can be included in the course itself.

Summaries of the subject areas are of little help if you are concerned about the development of skills and human resources. In this case it can be a good idea to skim through the book as a whole and concentrate on the Participants' Notes. However, the criterion is a difficult one to employ successfully. It requires above-average imagination and a considerable degree of open-mindedness. It is easy to be over-influenced by the subject matter. Ideally, one should look at all the events and not skip over those which, on first sight, seem to have no connection with the target skills. For example, if one is looking for events which could develop negotiating skills it would be easy to skip over DETECTIVE STORY, since the subject matter concerns a detective writer who has a mental block and the participants are thoughts in the author's mind who meet in pairs to try to get the story moving again. Yet since they have to agree on what story to suggest to their mind-blocked author this involves negotiation; not the type of negotiation in which two sides start from entrenched positions, but negotiation nevertheless, involving negotiation skills.

Another example is where one might be looking for supportive skills and close co-operation among participants. The tendency would be to concentrate on the simulations or exercises and ignore GROWING PAPER CLIPS in the chapter on games. Even to look at the description (people form chains each holding their own paper clips), might not suggest the close supportive, affective, and co-operative behaviour that results from this activity. So, if you are looking at skill areas, or emotional areas, then it is useful to imagine the event from the inside and say 'What would I actually do if I were involved in this event, and how would I react to what other people might do?'

Another method of choice, not to be despised, is to take random samplings of the book as a whole - just open the book anywhere and read that event. This can be valuable if you are not sure what the book has to offer, in which case preconceived ideas such as those mentioned above could have an undesirable effect in limiting your choice.

If you feel you ought to know what you want but are a bit vague about it, then you might like to draw up a list. Do you want the event to help people to:

1   match names to faces;
2   get to know each other on an intellectual problem-solving level;
3   find out how imaginative and/or humorous people are;
4   meet on the level of organizational efficiency (or inefficiency);
5   discover people's aptitudes in creative authorship;
6   seek personal friendships and warmth;
7   have formal contacts;
8   talk formally to colleagues and make short speeches;
9   reveal attitudes, views, beliefs, likes and dislikes;
10   display skills of journalism and presentation;
11   exhibit ability to critically analyse situations and problems?

It is easy to add to this list and then form a shortlist of priorities. Most of the events in this book combine several of the above features.

Social factors might also be considered. Do you want the participants to hurry around meeting each other? If so, it is probably better to pick a game rather than an exercise or simulation, since the desire to win will increase speed of movement. Most games in this book have some sort of time limit or deadline whereas the exercises and simulations are more open-ended. So if you prefer the more leisurely (civilized?) approach, then avoid the section on games. Similarly, if the normal social behaviour of the participants is keenly competitive - which in practice seems to mean that most of them are males - then that is a reason for choosing games, or avoiding games, depending on your general attitude.

Most people can cope fairly easily with routine situations but are less efficient when something unusual occurs. So if you want to encourage flexibility of mind look for the unusual, the imaginative and the creative.

Here are a few practical examples of the start of contrasting lists:

Imaginative	DETECTIVE STORY, WORKING SLOGANS
Routine	COINCIDENCES, UNIQUENESS
Open-ended	DESIGNING COUNTRIES, ROOM
One answer	MIXED WEDDING, RELATIVE LETTERS GAME
Business	CORPORATE IMAGE, MAGICIANS
Environment	DESIGNING COUNTRIES, ENDANGERED SPECIES
Personal	BIRTHDAY SCORES, BORING SKILLS
Non-personal	LOCK AND KEY, MIXED WEDDING

Other headings might be sociological/scientific, individuals/groups, authorship/reporting, real-world/fantasy. Anyway, drawing up lists can be fun, and should not be treated too seriously.

It may seem implicit in the above discussion that you should sit down in private with a pen and a blank sheet of paper and make your choice, after perhaps deciding the best way of doing it. However, this procedure seems to leave out a potentially vital question - namely 'Who should choose?' There are plenty of options. You could consult with your colleagues or with the trainees/students themselves. You could offer options. You could put it to the vote. You could even ask other people the question 'Who should choose?' Such a period of consultation with the trainees/students, even if only a five-minute discussion, could in itself reveal a range of attitudes and beliefs which contribute to the icebreaking process.

Another question, which should always be asked, is whether any icebreaker is suitable for the particular circumstances. The people concerned might be so competent, so single-minded, or so well known to each other outside the course or conference that they regard any icebreaker as a time-wasting nuisance. In that case, and assuming that you agree with them, you should have no hesitation in not using an icebreaker. However, you could still dip into the book to see if there are events which could fit into the course itself. In that case, just avoid the label 'icebreaker' when publicizing the event.

Finally, and perhaps most importantly, choice should depend on personal experience. Do try out a potentially useful event, don't just read the documents. Although I keep remarking that this book contains 'events', 'games', 'exercises' and 'simulations' this is really shorthand for saying 'contains the documents for these events'. Real events must happen. Games, exercises and simulations are not sheets of paper, or instructions, or rules - they are things that people do. So try to transform the printed word into action before the event itself takes place. Find one or two friends or colleagues and devote at least ten minutes to being a participant and using participatory language. Don't distance yourself as a judge. Don't say to your colleagues 'I would begin this activity by saying to you...' - just say it.

It is difficult to over-stress this point. Personal involvement, even briefly, is vital, and is time well spent. It will help you to envisage the layout of the furniture, the way to handle small or large numbers, to estimate the time needed, and it is likely to illuminate points that might seem unclear on first reading. It reveals important human dimensions which are not obvious from just reading the description of what the participants have to do. Also, personal participation will help you to distinguish the methodologies far better than just reading about differences.

For example, in GROWING PAPER CLIPS the players have to keep hold of their own paper clips. Just to read this instruction does not reveal the close proximity which occurs in practice when five or more players form a chain.

In MAGICIANS the word 'ethics' is not mentioned in the documents for the participants. It is easy to get the impression that the event will focus on magic and business efficiency. Yet all it takes is for someone to decide that their business is a casino, or a firm of stockbrokers, for the word 'unfair' to surface. In games, the only morality concerns cheating, but in simulations the participants carry around with them their own codes of ethics.

The two examples above are mentioned in the respective Facilitator's Notes, but there is no substitute for personal participation in order to get the feel of the event and to combat plausible but false expectations. The main problem with false expectations is that the facilitator may fail to perceive what actually happened and try to debrief the preconceived event rather than the actual one. With interactive learning events the unexpected occurs far more frequently than with instructional teaching, so it is important to cultivate an open mind.

How to run the icebreakers

As recommended, do try the event first. Then decide, in relation to the numbers involved, whether you may need any help. Should you ask the students for a volunteer assistant? Do you want to have an observer or two? Is there anyone you could consult about facilities? Can any colleagues come in to assist? You may even be in a situation in which it is beneficial that the event should be run by a student, or group of students, with you in the role of observer/adviser to the facilitator. These are all options worth considering.

The worst possible scenario is to read the documents hastily, photocopy a few which seem useful, and then rush into the room in a state of some uncertainty. This gives the impression that the event is of no consequence and probably suggests to the participants that you are not properly prepared, which will not inspire their confidence in you.

The briefing itself should be extremely brief. Just explain the mechanics regarding the timing and facilities and hand out the notes for the participants. Make sure, of course, to avoid inappropriate terminology, particularly beware of using 'game' or 'player' when introducing an exercise or simulation. This will help to avoid those unpleasant surprises which tend to accompany ambivalents.

However, there is an important alternative to handing out the notes at the beginning of the session. There are circumstances in which it would be beneficial to distribute them before the session begins. Perhaps they could be included in the pre-publicity materials for a conference, or enclosed in the documents handed out when people register for the course. In this way they would serve as an appetizer, help to avoid unnecessary apprehensions, give the participants time to work out some ideas, and allow a prompt start. Some working documents might also be enclosed with the notes but care should be taken not to 'give the game away'.

In all the events the Facilitator's Notes consists of six parts, and are brief, so here are few additional words of explanation and advice:

1. All the Facilitator's Notes start with a summary of the activity but in order to understand what is involved the notes should be read in conjunction with the notes for the participants. The two are interdependent. The assumption is that you will photocopy the notes for the participants and hand them out with a few words of explanation.

True, you could simply describe the instructions verbally and not bother about photocopying them, but this is dangerous. It is very easy to miss out vital points. To rely on the spoken word alone means that participants tend to forget parts of what was said, or misunderstand the situation despite the fact that the explanation may have been extremely lucid. They have one chance only to hear something, whereas when given the written word they can reread if they were distracted or failed to understand. To omit photocopying the notes in order to save time usually results in far more time being required later because some have filled in the wrong form, or have to spend time debating what they are supposed to be doing. This could lead to the facilitator having to intervene - leading to loss of 'realism' and damaging the intellectual and emotional feeling of participant autonomy which should be an essential ingredient of all icebreakers, and indeed all other similar interactive events.

2. Regarding numbers: this question should be considered in the context of the space and the facilities. When I say 'No maximum number' I mean that there can be as many participants as will fit reasonably happily into the space, and that can include extra rooms, a corridor, a garden. The furniture arrangements are something you should consider carefully before running an event. Icebreakers are intended to help people meet each other. So a room full of armchairs, or of desks nailed to the floor, may be an impediment to running the particular event you have chosen. It may be necessary, or useful, to move the furniture against the walls. Another consideration is confidentiality. Can the furniture be used to help preserve conditions of confidentiality in those events which require it? Can a corridor, garden, coffee shop, foyer, or even private cars be used for confidential negotiations?

3. The question of timing is somewhat different in icebreakers than in other interactive learning events. Since the aim is to meet people it is convenient to give an approximate time related to the number of participants. Meetings, if only for one minute each, take time. The times given in the Facilitator's Notes are dependent on how many people you want the participants to meet - all of them, most of them, or about half of them? As suggested in the last section, if you use a game then you are likely to spur people into making speedier contacts than if you use an exercise or simulation, although the quality (and politeness) of each

encounter might be somewhat abrupt. Also, the estimate of time is very rough - you should find out for yourself whether, with your participants and in your particular circumstances, you need more time or less time.

4. The section on materials does not refer to everyday objects such as pens. Special objects (paper clips) are specified, but facilitators should consider what other available items could be useful - clipboards, notice boards, tape recorders and cameras (preferably used for plausible reasons within the events), duplicating equipment, flat surfaces for writing, and even cups of tea or coffee - all depending on the nature of the event itself. To avoid needless repetition the materials section does not mention the notes for participants. It is assumed that these will be photocopied automatically. Another important point not mentioned is whether to make the copied documents more durable by sticking them onto cards. Clearly this will depend on circumstances.

5. The procedure for each event is described only briefly in the Facilitator's Notes, partly because additional details occur in the notes for participants and partly because the circumstances of events can vary so greatly it is difficult to give anything other than brief general guidance. However, it is always worth bearing in mind that the icebreakers are not taught events. Avoid guiding and hinting and coaching. Do not sit down next to the participants and ask them how they are getting on. Try to be invisible. Avoid answering a participant who asks for advice, as distinct from a question about the mechanics of the event.

6. Debriefing is a technical word which usually means a discussion after the event. Debriefings are unusual after running an icebreaker. Most books assume that there will be no subsequent discussion. This perhaps is another reason why icebreakers are treated so perfunctorily. Yet icebreakers are interactive events involving human beings and in all interactive events, including those in this book, the unpredictable sometimes happens. People can get emotional about what occurs. Although the separation of methodologies in this book will help eliminate emotions arising from participants operating on different methodological wavelengths, you should still think of a debriefing as a natural outlet for people to say what they think.

Some authorities on interactive events in general advocate having a debriefing which lasts at least twice as long as the event itself. My own view is that with these icebreakers a debriefing of five to ten minutes should be sufficient in most cases, unless the event has been brought into the course for reasons other than its icebreaking properties, in which case a longer debriefing could be contemplated.

The format for the debriefing should be considered, since many trainers and teachers are under the impression that the only format is for them to stand at the front and ask questions and then praise and criticize. Such debriefings can be excellent, but they can degenerate into chat dominated by a few individuals, or a situation in which some participants become furious or apathetic because they wanted to express their pent-up emotions and were given no chance of doing so. Other options to the 'pedant model' include a preliminary mini-debriefing in groups, or even a debriefing in which all the participants have a clipboard with a question (their own, or supplied) about the event and they become pollsters moving around and engaging in mutual interviews. Another idea is to discuss the form of debriefing before the event begins, perhaps mentioning some of the dangers referred to in the last paragraph. Such discussion could consider the question not only of the type of debriefing but also who should be in charge. Perhaps it could be one or two participants with the facilitator in the roles of reporter, observer and consultant.

How to adapt the icebreakers

All trainers and teachers adapt as part of their professional work and since circumstances are so important it is useful to bear adaptations in mind when considering these icebreakers.

There are two main sorts of adaptation. One is the slight tinkering here and there with the timing, the furniture and the materials. But a more profound change can occur if you switch methodologies - change a game into a simulation, or a simulation into an exercise, etc. This is not too difficult.

1. To change a game abandon the scoring mechanism
2. To change a simulation abandon the roles
3. To change an exercise introduce a scoring mechanism or roles.

If you compare three events in the book - RELATIVE LETTERS GAME, RELATIVE LETTERS EXERCISE, and RELATIVE LETTERS SIMULATION you will see that they are all based on the same idea but each is significantly different when seen from the point of view of the participants. The game has the concept of winning, the exercise has the concept of learning, the simulation has the concept of professional conduct.

Professional-type roles are essential to a simulation, whereas there are no such roles in games and exercises. It is true, of course, that games can include the functions of banker, dungeonmaster, umpire - but these are administrative roles, not the roles of players. Exercises can have some functional roles which are similar to those in simulations, but they are without the assumption of a genuine job. For example, exercises could have the function of 'leader', but in a simulation the leader would be an officer, a managing director, a president, and would assume the full powers and responsibilities implicit in that job. Also, exercises have direct instructions from author to problem-solver, whereas the documents in a simulation are usually more like the professional documents in the real world.

For a practical example of different methodologies as seen from the viewpoint of authors, compare four of the exercises in this book - EXERCISE PLAN, GAME PLAN, ICEBREAKER PLAN and SIMULATION PLAN. All are virtually identical in format. They are all exercises about authorship. But the questions on the respective Ideas Forms reveal distinctive features of each methodology.

For a fuller discussion about designing interactive learning events in general there are several books which cover the subject. Unfortunately, most set out specific step-by-step procedures as a linear assembly-line process. This is not usually the way authors work - although some academics seem to think it is. I recommend my own books (see bibliography) which all have sections on design.

2

Summaries

The games

BIRTHDAY SCORES is a game in which players compare birthdays and form into groups which score by (a) birthdays in different months, or (b) birthdays not more than 11 days apart.

DIVERSE POINTS is a game in which players accumulate as many points as possible by meeting in pairs and trying to reach agreement on how to divide 100 points between them in any of four proportions: 90/10, 80/20, 70/30, 60/40. Other divisions such as 50/50 are not permitted.

FIRST NAME TERMS is a game in which players try to form themselves into groups which have the largest number of letters, provided that no letter is repeated.

GROWING PAPER CLIPS is a game in which each player is given a paper clip (or some other linking device) and the aim is to achieve the highest score by judicious linking. The player in the middle of a chain receives a bonus point.

LOCK AND KEY is a game in which each player has a lock and key card in which the key will not fit the lock. The aim is (a) for players to match their own keys and locks and (b) to introduce players to each other whose keys and locks will match.

LOST DEFINITIONS is a game in which players individually write the definition of a word and how the word might be misheard (vacation misheard as vocation). The misheard words and the definitions of the original words are shuffled and players have the job of matching the two.

MAPVILLE is a game in which players meet in pairs and have the job of working out K's route from home to the park. All streets run either north-south or east-west. K never walks more than one block along any street on the way to the park and buys a sandwich at J's delicatessen.

NEW NAMES is a game in which players try to find out as many new names as possible while at the same time trying to restrict information about their own new names.

RELATIVE LETTERS GAME is a game in which players try to find out not only the answer but also the question. Each player receives an evidence card containing a single letter and there are four clue cards handed out by the facilitator for each 20 per cent of the evidence collected. There are also two clues (hints) hidden in the Players' Notes.

SMALL WORLD is a game in which players exchange brief stories of the 'It's a small world' type, and have to guess whether the stories are fact or fiction.

TAKEOVER is a game in which each player starts as the owner of a company containing one of three words - aces, kings or twos. When a company is taken over the staff of that company receive jobs one step lower in the hierarchy.

TOUGH MAZE is a game in which players each receive a segment of a maze and have to meet in pairs, show each other their segments, and try to work out the whole of the maze. Altogether there are nine segments labelled T-O-U-G-H-M-A-Z-E in random order. Each segment overlaps with two, three or four other segments.

VALUEGRAMS is a game in which players try to form a (dictionary) word of not more than six letters in length, each letter taken from a different player, with a preliminary co-operative round to allocate numerical values to most of the letters in each name.

WINNING LINES is a game based on the nine-square matrix of Noughts and Crosses (Tic-Tac-Toe).

The exercises

CHARITABLE INTENTIONS is an exercise in which pairs design new charities, and seek opinions about their viability.

COINCIDENCES is an exercise in which pairs exchange information about themselves and try to find coincidences and estimate probabilities.

CORPORATE IMAGE is an exercise in which pairs form their own corporation, company or institution, choose three attributes they do not need for the corporate image, and then exchange these attributes with corporations which want these to help boost their corporate image.

ENDANGERED SPECIES is an exercise in which participants are given the names of a species (imaginary) and have to invent habitat, appearance and behaviour and then collect comments about the invented species.

EXERCISE PLAN is an exercise in which groups interchange members and take part in the step-by-step design of an exercise.

GAME PLAN is an exercise in which groups interchange members and take part in the step-by-step design of a game.

HALF A VOTE is an exercise in which everyone has half a vote. The aim is to combine two halves into one, and decide on a topic and forum for using the vote. Groups grow larger if there is consensus.

ICEBREAKER PLAN is an exercise in which groups interchange members and take part in the step-by-step design of an icebreaker.

'IS' IN THE MIDDLE is an exercise in which the participants devise their own sayings of not more than five words taken from a list, with each saying containing 'is' somewhere about the middle. Participants meet in pairs to try to match sayings with authors.

MIXED WEDDING is an exercise in which the participants have different pieces of information about a wedding. The problem is to find out who is the bride, groom, best man and bridesmaid, what their jobs are, and what they are wearing.

NEW TAXES is an exercise in inventing new taxes which would help to improve the quality of life or improve efficiency in general.

OLOGY is an exercise to invent, define and comment on new 'ologies'.

RELATIVE LETTERS EXERCISE is an exercise in which participants try to find out not only the answer but also the question. Each receives an evidence card containing a single letter and there are four clue cards handed out by the facilitator for each 20 per cent of the evidence collected. There are also two hints hidden in the Participants' Notes.

ROOM is an exercise involving a room. But the problem concerning the room, and a practical solution, must be deduced from the evidence.

SIMULATION PLAN is an exercise in which groups interchange members and take part in the step-by-step design of a simulation.

STARTING AGAIN is an exercise about options at birth - the choice being a trade-off between natural ability and parental income.

UNIQUENESS is an exercise in the unusual. Each participant writes down something unique about themselves. These cards are then shuffled and handed out, and participants have to compile a matching list.

WORKING SLOGANS is an exercise in which pairs invent an organization and choose a slogan, but the slogan is implemented by others.

The simulations

ARTIFACTS is a simulation set in the distant future where a virus in the computer network has destroyed all records and a group of sociologists, historians and scientists try to find the use for some ancient artifacts known as coin, key, pen, etc.

ARTISTIC SHAPES is a simulation in which participants alternate between being wall mural designers and specialists in drawing ovals or rectangles.

BORING SKILLS is a simulation about recruitment to an agency which has been required to provide skilled personnel for a luxury round-the-world cruise. The particular skill is to be an effective bore.

CAPTIONS is a simulation concerning the annual convention of RAPS (Reporters, Authors and Photographers Society) where delegates are keen to photograph each other and write captions for their pictures which they hope will be included in *Rapture*, the journal of the society.

DESIGNING COUNTRIES is a simulation in which the participants work in groups to design their own countries and welcome visitors.

DETECTIVE STORY is a simulation in which the participants are ideas for characters in an unwritten detective story in the mind of a famous author who has a mental block. The block prevents the ideas from joining together as a group - participants meet in pairs to try to get the story moving again.

FAIRGROUND is a simulation in which each participant keeps switching roles from that of a fairground owner who is planning a new fairground to that of a company which manufactures fairground features - rides, slides, shows, etc.

FORWARD TO THE PAST is a simulation in which participants are scriptwriters who have to devise a story to fit the title.

LAUGH LAUGHING, INC. is a simulation about a publishing house of that name which publishes joke books and is contemplating changing its name, policy and image.

MAGICIANS is a simulation in which members of the Magnificent Guild of Magicians are interviewed by various organizations to see if they can be offered short-term contracts.

MONOLITH is a simulation in which the participants are archaeologists and sociologists who have to theorize about a round stone object that has been found in a clearing in a jungle in a South American country.

MOTIVATE is a simulation about organizations with the problem of staff who are insufficiently motivated. The participants are executives who have been asked to come up with ideas.

PERSONAL ENDORSEMENTS is a simulation involving surveys of the potential value of some new uses for old or used objects.

RELATIVE LETTERS SIMULATION is a simulation involving scientists seeking theories and funds regarding the relationship of certain letters.

WORRIED is a simulation in which a 'worried' pair seek advice from a pair who, on request, take the roles of fortune tellers, or personnel counsellors, or management consultants, or human rights advisers.

ZAP is a simulation involving space officers and potential danger from strange creatures on the outer surface of a distant planet.

3

Methodology

What are we supposed to do and why?

Games, exercises and simulations are not only different from each other, they are incompatible. If some people treat an event as a game while others behave as if it were an exercise or simulation then the result will be disappointing, or unpleasant, or even disastrous. It is important to know what methodology you are supposed to be in.

Games

Chess, bridge, football, darts and Monopoly are all games, and their distinguishing features are (a) they all have a scoring mechanism to determine the winner and (b) they are all closed events in which their rules require no outside justification. Thus, no one in Monopoly says 'You should not knock down houses in order to build hotels - what about the homeless people?' In football no one says 'This effort to score is highly inefficient and it would be much more productive if there was only one team'. To criticize any game 'Because it is not like real life' is to make a mistake of category. In a game there is only one role, that of player, and a player has a duty to try to win according to the rules. It is as simple as that.

Exercises

These are events in which there are no roles except those of problem-solvers or decision-makers. If the exercise is in the nature of a puzzle the participants would say 'I solved it' or 'I could not work it out' rather than 'I won' or 'I lost'. What matters is a duty to try to solve the problem. Solvers and puzzlers do not usually receive points, otherwise the event would probably be a game.

Simulations

These are misnamed events in the sense that the participants do not simulate. It is the environment that is simulated. A simulation is not a drama. Playacting is out, and participants do not have a personality transplant. But they do receive new functions and duties - journalists, managers, artists, etc. They do not pretend to be these things - they are journalists because they write news stories, managers because they manage, and artists because they engage in artistic creation. Their efforts are rarely professional in expertise, but they do have to be professional in intention.

4

The games

Birthday Scores is a game in which players compare birthdays and form into groups which score by (a) birthdays in different months, or (b) birthdays not more than 11 days apart.

Numbers: The minimum number of players is probably about eight. There is no maximum number.

Time: Allow about five minutes for the players to read the PLAYERS' NOTES, add one minute for each player, and that can be the time limit. For example, with 25 players the time allowed could be half an hour.

Materials: BIRTHDAY CARDS (one for each player) and the GROUP LIST (about one list for every three players).

Procedure: Arrange for a notice board or some other means of 'publishing' the GROUP LISTS, perhaps by displaying them on a table or sticking them on a wall. Hand out the PLAYERS' NOTES and BIRTHDAY CARDS, one for each player. Show the players your pile of GROUP LISTS and tell them that they are available as required. Announce the deadline.

Debriefing: Since the action may be somewhat confusing with different groups operating under different scoring systems it could be useful to start the debriefing by asking the players what happened to themselves and to their groups. The next part of the debriefing can depend upon the answers and the circumstances of the course (conference, class).

Birthday Scores is a game in which players compare birthdays and form into groups which score by (a) birthdays in different months, or (b) birthdays not more than 11 days apart.

MONTHS	DAYS (a two-player group)
3 in different months 3 points each	born 11 days apart 1 point each
4 in different months 4 points each	born 10 days apart 2 points each
5 in different months 5 points each	born 9 days apart 3 points each
6 in different months 6 points each	born 8 days apart 4 points each
7 in different months 7 points each	born 7 days apart 5 points each
and so on until	and so on until
12 in different months 12 points each	born on same day 12 points each

If counting by days the individual scores are doubled for each additional member of the group.   If three players were born on the same day they would score 24 points each, four players 48 points each.   The span is based on the two outer days, so a three-player group born on the 1st, 4th, and 8th of a particular month all have birthdays within a span of seven days which is ten points each (five points doubled).   Where relevant, 29th February is counted as a day. Year endings are ignored.

Begin by writing your name and birthday (but not the year) on your BIRTHDAY CARD. Information gathering must be done privately between two parties (two singles, a single and a group, two groups) who must first introduce themselves. Three or more parties are not allowed to meet together. Players who announce or disclose their birthdays in public are disqualified.

A group is formed by devising a geographical title (Alaska, Zambia, etc), writing in the names of its members on a GROUP LIST and 'publishing' it. The list must not disclose the birthdays or the method of scoring. A group can divide and gather information separately. Joining (or rejoining) a group requires the permission of all its members. Leaving a group needs no permission, but the leaver must tell the group before doing so and the name must be removed from the old list before being added to a new list.   At the end of the game the group with the highest score wins.

BIRTHDAY SCORES

Birthday Cards

(cut out the ten cards)

Birthday Card Name................................... Day .... Month	**Birthday Card** Name................................... Day .... Month ....
Birthday Card Name................................... Day .... Month	**Birthday Card** Name................................... Day .... Month ....
Birthday Card Name................................... Day .... Month	**Birthday Card** Name................................... Day .... Month ....
Birthday Card Name................................... Day .... Month	**Birthday Card** Name................................... Day .... Month ....
Birthday Card Name................................... Day .... Month	**Birthday Card** Name................................... Day .... Month ....

BIRTHDAY SCORES

Group name ....

_____

_____

_____

_____

_____

_____

_____

_____

_____

K. Jones 1992, published by Kogan Page

Diverse Points is a game in which players accumulate as many points as possible by meeting in pairs and trying to reach agreement on how to divide 100 points between them in any of four proportions: 90/10, 80/20, 70/30, 60/40. Other divisions such as 50/50 are not permitted.

Numbers: The minimum number is probably six and the maximum number is limited only by the size of the room.

Time: It may be a good idea to set a deadline based on five minutes for reading the PLAYERS' NOTES and then one minute for each player. Thus, with 25 players you could set a time limit of half an hour. Announce the time limit before the game begins and give a five-minute and a one-minute warning as the deadline approaches.

Materials: POINTS LIST, one for each player.

Procedure: Divide the room into two separate areas with a clearly marked frontier - chalk line, row of chairs, etc. Label one area the Negotiation Area and the other area the Leisure Area. Assemble the players in the Leisure Area and hand out to all players the PLAYERS' NOTES and the POINTS LIST. If there are more than 20 participants then work out in advance how you will organize the group at the end of the game so as to facilitate the announcements of the scores.

Debriefing: In any debriefing a major point is likely to be the negotiation skills and the strategies. For example, if two greedy players meet then their overall scores are likely to be on the low side because the time they spend disagreeing will reduce the number of negotiations they can complete. Compare the strategies of the high-score players with those of the low-score players. Some players may be unhappy that a 50/50 division is prohibited, so one item for discussion is whether the game is unfair in some way.

Diverse Points is a game in which players accumulate as many points as possible by meeting in pairs and trying to reach agreement on how to divide 100 points between them in any of four proportions: 90/10, 80/20, 70/30, 60/40. Other divisions such as 50/50 are not permitted.

Begin by writing your own name at the bottom of the POINTS LIST. The first column of the LIST is for you to write in the name of the player you are negotiating with. The second column is for the points the other player awards you. If you fail to agree then you write 0 in this column. If you reach agreement then write in one number only, for example if you are awarded 70 then write down 70 and not 70/30 or 30/70. The third column is for the other player's signature to confirm the figure written in the second column.

The Leisure Area is for single players to form pairs in preparation for negotiation. No negotiations of any sort are permitted in the Leisure Area.

The Negotiations Area is reserved for negotiations, Only pairs can enter the Negotiations Area. If a player wants to conceal information about previous deals then the POINTS LIST can be folded to reveal only free lines plus the player's name at the bottom. A negotiation (whatever the result) is complete when both players have added their signatures to the LISTS and not before. The pair must return immediately to the Leisure Area.

The game ends at the deadline and any incomplete paperwork does not count. The player with the highest total score wins.

DIVERSE POINTS

Points List

I negotiated with	who awarded me	signed by

Name ....

K. Jones 1992, published by Kogan Page

First Name Terms is a game in which the players try to form themselves into groups which have the largest number of letters on their FIRST NAME CARDS, provided that no letter is repeated.

Numbers: The minimum number is probably six or seven, and there is no maximum.

Time: It may be a good idea to allow five minutes for players to sort themselves out then add one minute for each player and announce this as the deadline. Thus, 15 players could be allocated 20 minutes.

Materials: FIRST NAME CARDS (one for each participant) and the GROUP LISTS (one for every two participants).

Procedure: Hand out the FIRST NAME CARDS, probably at the same time as you hand out the PLAYERS' NOTES. Show the players the GROUP LISTS and explain that these will be kept in a pile and made available on request. Allow time for the players to read the NOTES and fill in their FIRST NAME CARDS.

Debriefing: Depending on circumstances any debriefing will probably include a discussion of strategies. How efficient were they? How polite were they? Would they do it differently if the game was restarted with another group of players? Another element is humour - did the participants invent interesting group names, perhaps matching their personalities? Did anyone have creative ideas?

K. Jones 1992, published by Kogan Page

First Name Terms is a game in which players try to form themselves into groups which have the largest number of letters, provided that no letter is repeated.

Write your first name (long or short version as you prefer) on your FIRST NAME CARD, plus a second version leaving out any recurring letter. Thus Adam would be written Adm, Eve becomes Ev, and Otto becomes Ot. Michael could choose whether to be Michael or Mike but once written on the FIRST NAME CARD it cannot be altered subsequently.

Each letter is counted as one, and each player's score is their own score plus the group's total score. If a group consisted of Adm, Ev and Ot the group score would be seven (3+2+2). Adm would score ten (7+3) while Ev and Ot would each score nine (7+2). Michael could not join Adm or Ev because of recurring letters. Mike could join Adm but not Ev.

Each potential group must give itself the name of a well-known author of any type of literature - Hemingway, Shakespeare, Barrie etc. Groups do not have official existence until the names of their members (as shown on the FIRST NAME CARDS) are written on one of the GROUP LISTS (see the facilitator) and stuck on the wall or on a board. Group existence occurs with publication and not before.

No group can accept a new member unless all existing members agree to this. However, a player can leave a group without the agreement of any of its members. Joining or leaving a group takes effect from the moment when the player's name is added to or deleted from the published GROUP LIST. If a list should shrink to one player (or none) it remains on public display but must be marked 'Defunct'. If, at the end of the game, a player's name is on two lists, then the player is disqualified and the scores of both groups recalculated accordingly.

At the end of the game the winner is the player with the highest score.

(cut out)

First Name Card

My first name is ....

Without
recurring letters　...............................

First Name Card

My first name is ....

Without
recurring letters　...............................

First Name Card

My first name is ....

Without
recurring letters　...............................

First Name Card

My first name is ....

Without
recurring letters　...............................

First Name Card

My first name is ....

Without
recurring letters　...............................

First Name Card

My first name is ....

Without
recurring letters　...............................

K. Jones 1992, published by Kogan Page

Group name ....

Group members

_____

_____

_____

_____

_____

GROWING PAPER CLIPS   FACILITATOR'S NOTES

Growing Paper Clips is a game in which players each have a paper clip and the aim is to achieve the highest score by the judicious linking of paper clips. The player in the middle of a chain receives a bonus point.

Numbers:
The minimum number is probably six and the maximum number is limited only by the size of the room.

Time:
Set a time limit for the game, perhaps one minute for each player up to a 30-minute limit. Announce the deadline and give a five-minute and a one-minute warning before the deadline is reached

Materials:
Paper clips (or key rings, or any other interlocking devices) are the only required materials, with one paper clip for each player plus about 10 per cent extra in case of breakages.

Procedure:
Hand out the PLAYERS' NOTES to each player, and perhaps at the same time give each player their paper clip. You could emphasize the point that each player is responsible for the safety of their own clip, but should it get damaged then they can get a new clip from you at the cost of losing a point at the end of the game.

Debriefing:
Depending on circumstances a key issue is likely to be the tone and the effectiveness of the negotiations and strategies. Was it better for singles to join singles or to join pairs; better to be cautious or better to act quickly? How polite were the players? Did anyone have any bright ideas? How did the players feel about joining or not joining? Remember that most players will have treated the activity as an icebreaker game and the facilitator should not try to judge it as a personality assessment test. Should any players be upset by something that happened in the game or something that is said in the debriefing then allow time for them to make their points and allow time for other people to reply.

K. Jones 1992, published by Kogan Page

Growing Paper Clips is a game in which each player is given a paper clip (or some other linking device) and the aim is to achieve the highest score by judicious linking. The player in the middle of a chain receives a bonus point.

All chains must have an odd number of members, except for a pair. This means that two pairs cannot join together, nor can two odd-numbered chains, since the result would be an even-numbered chain. Two singles can join together only by mutual consent. A single player can join a pair at any time and decide which end to join, whether the members of the pair agree or not, but a pair cannot join a single player unless that player agrees. Similarly, a pair can join a larger group at any time and decide which end to join, but a larger group cannot join a pair unless the pair agrees. Each linkage is a separate event, so three singles (or three chains) cannot join together simultaneously.

A player who does not join a chain automatically receives a special score of five points. Individual scores for players in chains are the same as the size of the chain with the player in the middle scoring a bonus point. In a chain of three the two outer players would score three and the middle player would score four. With a chain of 19 players all would score 19 except for the tenth player in the line who would score 20. In a pair there is no middle player, so each would score two points.

A chain must be a single straight line. It must not be a circle and it must not have branches. With each linkage, even when two singles form a pair, each player (newcomers and existing members) must
  (a) introduce themselves and
  (b) say what they personally hope to get out of the new chain - information, friendship, a polite chat, a good score, etc.

No players can leave a chain. All players must retain hold of their own paper clips. No player must take hold of any paper clip other than their own. Should a player's paper clip become damaged then a new one can be obtained from the facilitator at the cost of one point being deducted from that player's final score. At the end of the game all linkages must be demonstrably intact in order to score.

LOCK AND KEY   FACILITATOR'S NOTES

Lock and Key is a game in which each player has a LOCK AND KEY
CARD in which the key will not fit the lock. The aim is (a) for players to match
their own keys and locks and (b) to introduce players to each other whose lock
and key will match.

Numbers: The minimum number is nine and there is no maximum.

Time: Allow one or two minutes for each player.

Materials: One copy for each player of a LOCK AND KEY CARD, a
JOTTINGS SHEET, and a SCORE CARD. Each sheet of LOCK AND KEY
CARDS has three cards which match completely, making a total of 12 cards.
With 13 or more players just hand out extra cards and those players who find
they have identical cards will merge into one player. With exactly 10 (or 11)
players use only the first three sheets (9 cards) and add one (or two) extra cards
from the first sheet. Otherwise, if you use one or two cards only from the fourth
sheet there will be at least one player who will have no lock for the key, or no
key for the lock.

Procedure: Cut out the cards before the game but keep them in their sets,
otherwise there is a danger of failing to hand out a complete set of twelve.
Hand out the PLAYERS' NOTES , JOTTINGS SHEETS and the SCORE
CARDS. Place the LOCK AND KEY CARDS face downwards and allow the
players to pick their own - this demonstrates that the distribution is fair and
helps to preserve secrecy.

Debriefing: Decide in advance how to find out individual scores after the
game - perhaps asking the players to take it in turn to announce their own
scores. The winner is likely to be the player with a natural ability to remember
shapes and visualize orientations, but some players may have evolved successful
strategies for jotting down the combinations of shapes, and this area might be
worth exploring.

           K. Jones 1992, published by Kogan Page

Lock and Key is a game in which each player has a LOCK AND KEY CARD in which the key will not fit the lock. The aim is (a) for players to match their own keys and locks with those of other players and (b) to introduce players to each other whose keys and locks will match.

Write your name on your three documents - LOCK AND KEY CARD, JOTTINGS SHEET and SCORE CARD. Take reasonable precautions to keep your own LOCK AND KEY CARD secret. The JOTTINGS SHEET is to help you keep track of other people's locks and keys.

You must meet only in pairs, and privately, except when a player is introducing two other players to each other. Four or more players must never meet. Players must keep a record of their meeting by writing down the names of the people they meet, plus any score (or minus score) which results from the meeting.

If two players find they have an identical LOCK AND KEY card they must merge into the same player, and stick together.

You score five points when your key matches another player's lock or the other way round, even though you might have been introduced to each other by a third player. If you introduce two players to each other and they achieve a match then you score ten points, but if the match proves to be incorrect then you lose five points.

At the end of the game the winner is the player with the most points.

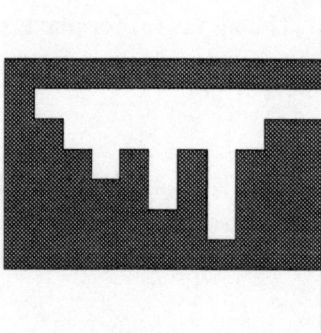 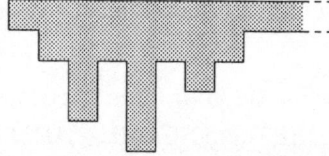

Name ....

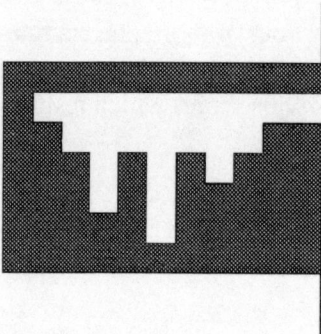 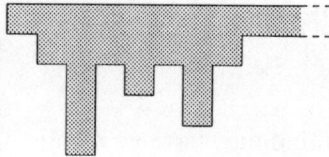

Name ....

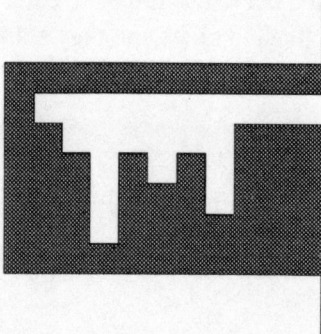 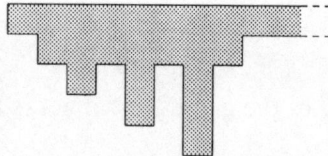

Name ....

K. Jones 1992, published by Kogan Page

Lock and Key Cards (page 2)
(cut out)

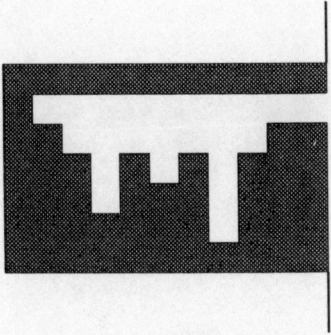 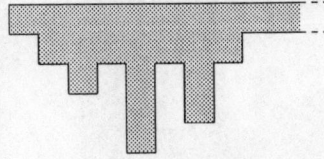

Name ....

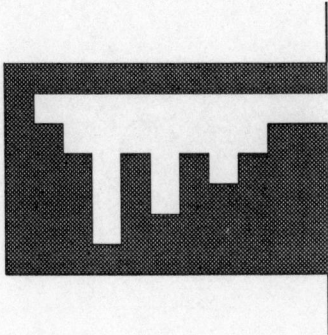 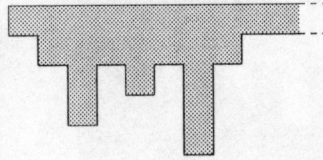

Name ....

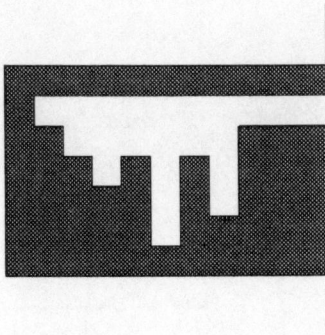 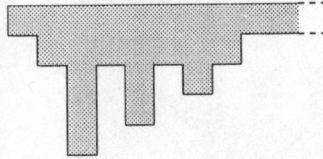

Name ....

Lock and Key Cards (page 3)
(cut out)

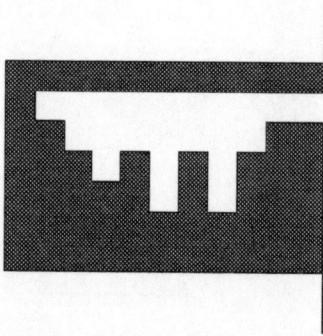 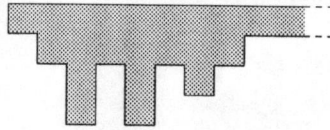

Name ....

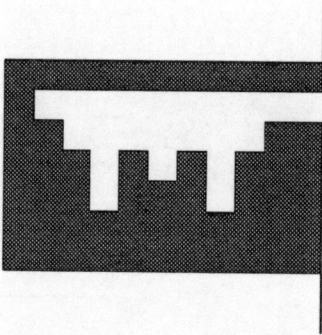 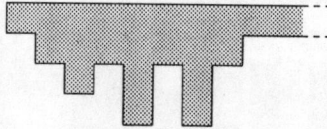

Name ....

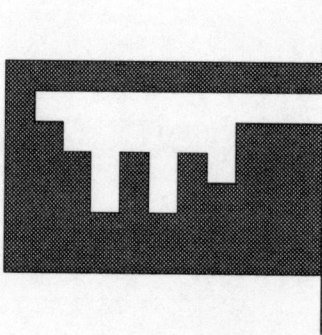 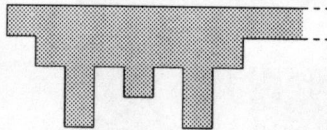

Name ....

K. Jones 1992, published by Kogan Page

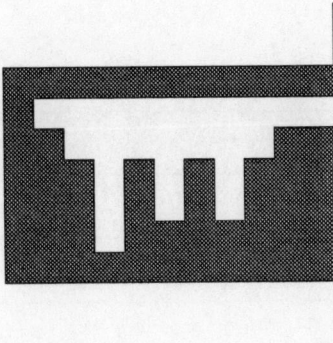 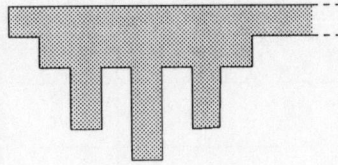

Name ....

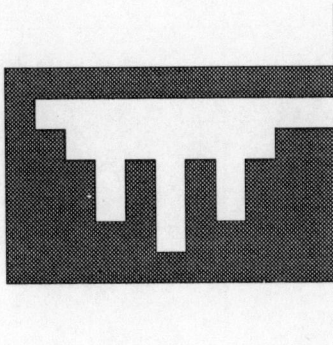 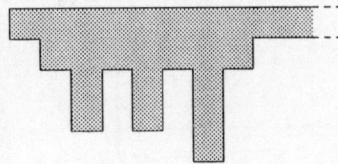

Name ....

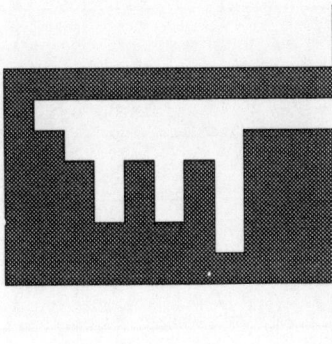 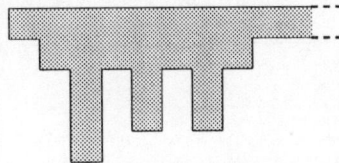

Name ....

LOCK AND KEY

Jottings Sheet

Name ....

player	lock	key

K. Jones 1992, published by Kogan Page

LOCK AND KEY

Score Card

Name ....

Met player	Score	INTRODUCED Player to Player		Score

Lost Definitions is a game in which players individually write the definition of a word and how the word might be misheard (for example, vacation misheard as vocation). The misheard words and the definitions of the original words are shuffled. Players have the job of matching the two.

Numbers: The minimum number is about six. There is no maximum.

Time: Ten minutes, plus about two minutes for each player.

Materials: One copy for each player of the WORD CARD, DEFINITION CARD, and DICTIONARY SHEET.

Procedure: Hand out one copy for each player of the PLAYERS' NOTES plus a copy to each player of the WORD CARD, DEFINITION CARD and DICTIONARY SHEET. Set a time limit for players to fill in their WORD CARDS and DEFINITION CARDS and ask that they be handed in to you. Check that players hand you the correct card. They should give you the misheard word (bottom of card) and keep the original word (top of card). The two packs of misheard words and definitions should be shuffled separately and placed face down for players to pick one from each pack.

Lost Definitions is a game in which players individually write the definition of a word and how the word might be misheard (for example, vacation misheard as vocation). The misheard words and the definitions of the original words are shuffled. Players have the job of matching the two.

Think of two words, preferably two nouns, that sound similar (path/bath, prince/prints). Then define one of the words and write this on your DEFINITION CARD. Write the word itself at the top of the WORD CARD with the misheard version at the bottom. Tear the card in two and keep (for reference) the original word. (Don't mix up the cards.) Hand the misheard word, together with your definition of the original word, to the facilitator.

You will receive at random a MISHEARD WORD and a DEFINITION. It does not matter if either, or even both, are you own, just copy them onto your DICTIONARY SHEET, but on different lines - unless, of course, they match. Move around and meet in pairs and show your MISHEARD WORD and DEFINITION CARD. Copy the misheard word and definition shown by the other players onto your DICTIONARY SHEET. You could keep this confidential by folding it. If the list already contains the definition 'A royal person' and if you come upon the misheard word 'prints' then you can match the two.

At the end of the game the player whose list contains the most correct matches is the winner.

(cut out)

Word Card

Original word

....

.... fold and tear here.........

Word misheard as

....

Word Card

Original word

....

.... fold and tear here.........

Word misheard as

....

Word Card

Original word

....

.... fold and tear here.........

Word misheard as

....

Word Card

Original word

....

.... fold and tear here.........

Word misheard as

....

Word Card

Original word

....

.... fold and tear here.........

Word misheard as

....

Word Card

Original word

....

.... fold and tear here.........

Word misheard as

....

K. Jones 1992, published by Kogan Page

Definition card	Definition of original word
....	

Definition card	Definition of original word
....	

Definition card	Definition of original word
....	

Definition card	Definition of original word
....	

Definition card	Definition of original word
....	

Definition card	Definition of original word
....	

Definition card	Definition of original word
....	

Definition card	Definition of original word
....	

LOST DEFINITIONS

Dictionary Sheet

Player	Misheard word	Definition of original word

K. Jones 1992, published by Kogan Page

Mapville is a game in which players meet in pairs and have the job of working out K's route from home to the park. All streets run north-south or east-west. K never walks more than one block along any street on the way to the park (K's general progress being diagonal) and K stops to buy a cheese and salad sandwich at J's delicatessen.

Numbers: the minimum number is nine - one CLUE CARD each. With 10 to 13 players hand out the optional CLUE CARDS - one card each. With 14 or more just start with a new sheet of CLUE CARDS. If two players find they have an identical card they merge into the same player and stick together. There is no maximum number.

Time: Allow about two minutes for each player.

Materials: A set of 13 CLUE CARDS to be cut out. One GRID and STREET NAMES LIST for each player.

Procedure: Before the game cut out the CLUE CARDS keeping them in their original groups of nine and four. This procedure allows you to make sure that the nine cards always stay as a complete set and are not accidentally exchanged for any spare optional cards. Hand out the PLAYERS' NOTES, the GRID and the STREET NAMES LIST. Finally, allocate the CLUE CARDS in conditions of secrecy, perhaps placing them face down on a table and allowing the players to choose their own.

Debriefing: Arrange for some procedure whereby players can announce their answers. The correct answer is: Lodge, Hyde, Kensington, Sunset, Deborah, Ruth. In discussing the problem you could point out that the position of the delicatessen should have been located before deciding whether K should travel west along Ashdown or south along Lodge. Although both routes reach the park, only the Lodge route passes the delicatessen.

Mapville is a game in which players meet in pairs and have the job of working out K's route from home to the park. In MAPVILLE all streets run either north-south or east-west. K never walks more than one block along any street on the way to the park (K's general progress being diagonal) and K stops to buy a cheese and salad sandwich at J's delicatessen.

Begin by writing your name on the CLUE CARD, GRID and STREET NAMES LIST.

Players meet in pairs (never in groups of three or larger) and must show each other their CLUE CARD. The GRID is for jotting down notes or street names and should be kept folded to prevent accidental disclosure.

If you meet someone with an identical CLUE CARD you merge into the same player and must stick together.

The STREET NAMES LIST is the official entry for the puzzle. Write nothing on this LIST until you have worked out the full answer - make sure it works first on your GRID. Then show the LIST to the facilitator. The first player to submit the correct answer is the winner, but no second guesses are allowed.

K. Jones 1992, published by Kogan Page

(Cut out the CLUE CARDS - two pages)

Name

....

K's house is at the intersection
of Ashdown and Lodge

Name

....

The park entrance is at the
corner of Ruth and Norwood

Name

....

J's delicatessen is at the intersection
of Sunset and Kensington

Name

....

Deborah is immediately
east of Norwood

Name

....

Kensington is immediately
east of Deborah

Name

....

Ashdown is immediately
north of Hyde

Name

....

Kensington is immediately
west of Lodge

Name

....

Sunset is immediately
south of Hyde

(cut out the Clue Cards)

Name

....

Ruth is immediately
south of Sunset

(These last four cards are optional)

Name

....

Cambridge is immediately
north of Ashdown

Name

....

University is immediately
east of Lodge

Name

....

City is immediately
south of Ruth

Name

....

Bay is immediately
west of Norwood

K. Jones 1992, published by Kogan Page

MAPVILLE

Name ....

NOTES..

....

....

....

Player's name.................................

On the first line write down the name (one word only) of the
first street that K walked along for one block.   On the second
line write down the next street that K walked along for one
block.   And so on until K reached the park.

Do not write anything on this list until you have worked out the
whole of the route on the GRID.

_____

_____

_____

_____

_____

_____

_____

New Names is a game in which players try to find out as many new names as possible while at the same time trying to restrict information about their own new name.

Numbers: The minimum is probably five. There is no maximum.

Time: Allow one or two minutes for each player.

Materials: One copy per player of the NAMES LIST and IDENTITY CARD.

Procedure: Try to arrange for areas (corridors?) where players can meet with reasonable protection from deliberate or accidental espionage. Before the game begins it might be useful to point out to the players that they must not write their own new name on their NAMES LIST, since this can quickly ruin the game.

Debriefing: Make some arrangements (preferably in advance) for finding out the scores afterwards. You might ask 'Who found out ten new names?' and if only player A achieved this then ask 'How many discovered A's new name?' Work out A's score, and so on. The game has obvious parallels with the real world where some individuals and organizations wish to learn as much as possible while revealing as little as possible. If interesting results occur it could be worth exploring what happened. However, remember that the event was an icebreaker game, not a psychological test.

New Names is a game in which players try to find out as many new names as possible while at the same time trying to restrict information about their own new names. Each player needs an IDENTITY CARD (to be folded so that the names are on the outside) plus a NAMES LIST.

Write your real name in capital letters on the Real Name side of your IDENTITY CARD and invent a one-word name and write it in capital letters on the New Name side of the card. The invented name can be any name provided it is not too difficult to spell.

  Permitted: Hamlet, Biscuit, Betty, Napoleon, George, Washington.
  Not Permitted: Betty Biscuit, George Washington, Quocquackxy.

Players must meet only in pairs, privately, never in threes or larger groups. At all meetings players must reveal their real names, and must always write the other player's real name on their NAMES LIST. At the first meeting a player must also reveal the new name (the other side of the IDENTITY CARD), but is under no obligation to do so at any subsequent meetings. If a meeting between players A and B is the first for both, then both must reveal both their real and their new names. But if B then meets C and it is C's first meeting then C must reveal both sides of the IDENTITY CARD but player B is not obliged to reveal B's new name to C.

Players can reveal other people's new names if they so wish, perhaps by showing their NAMES LIST, or showing part of their NAMES LIST (folded), or by simply saying 'X's new name is such-and-such'. Waiting (hovering) close to a pair is not allowed. Players should take reasonable precautions against deliberate or accidental spying.

At the end of the game you score three points for each correct link on your NAMES LIST, and you lose two points for each player who has linked your real name with your new name on their list.

K. Jones 1992, published by Kogan Page

Identity Card

My real name is

....
.... fold here ....

My NEW name is

....

Identity Card

My real name is

....
.... fold here ....

My NEW name is

....

Identity Card

My real name is

....
.... fold here ....

My NEW name is

....

Identity Card

My real name is

....
.... fold here ....

My NEW name is

....

Players	New names

RELATIVE LETTERS GAME FACILITATOR'S NOTES

Relative Letters Game is a game in which players try to find out not only the answer but also the question. Each player receives an EVIDENCE CARD containing a single letter and there are four clue cards handed out by the facilitator for each 20 per cent of the evidence collected. There are also two clues (hints) hidden in the PLAYERS' NOTES.

Numbers: The minimum number is about six. There is no maximum.

Time: Allow about two minutes for each player.

Materials: RESEARCH AND THEORY SHEET - one for each player. CLUE CARDS - one sheet (12 cards) for every three players. EVIDENCE CARDS - one sheet (12 cards) for every ten players. The reason for having more EVIDENCE CARDS than players is that it is important to have undistributed cards so that the players can assume, if they wish to do so, that other letters, probably including E, are on the undistributed cards.

Procedure: Hand out the PLAYERS' NOTES the RESEARCH AND THEORY SHEETS and lay face down the EVIDENCE CARDS at random to be picked up by the players. Keep the CLUE CARDS in piles to be handed out when the requisite percentage of evidence has been obtained.

Debriefing: The extra clues in the PLAYERS' NOTES are the words 'theory' and 'relative', suggesting that the answer might have something to do with Einstein's Theory of Relativity, which is $E=mc^2$. To find the answer before the game ends count up the 'm' and 'c' cards remaining and deduct these two totals from the total numbers of 'm' and 'c' cards before the game began. Square the number of 'c' cards distributed to the players and multiply it by the number of their 'm' cards. With eight players (say 6 m and 2 c) the answer is two squared (four) multiplied by six which equals 24. If no one had heard of mc^2, or even not heard of the Theory of Relativity, it does not matter, they were just pre-Einstein, and their research and theories can be judged accordingly. The discussion can begin with problem-solving ideas. How did the winner (if there was one) arrive at the solution?

RELATIVE LETTERS GAME   PLAYERS' NOTES

The Relative Letters Game is a game in which players try to find out not only the answer but also the question. Each player receives an EVIDENCE CARD containing a single letter and there are four clue cards handed out by the facilitator for each 20 per cent of the evidence collected. There are also two clues (hints) hidden in these PLAYERS' NOTES.

You meet only in pairs, privately, never in threes or more. Apart from having to disclose your EVIDENCE CARD, you may reveal as much of your knowledge or theories as you wish.

There are four CLUE CARDS.   After you have obtained 20 per cent of the evidence - that is having met 20 per cent of the players - ask the facilitator for CLUE CARD ONE. On 40 per cent ask for CLUE CARD TWO, on 60 per cent ask for the third card, and ask for CLUE CARD FOUR when you have 80 per cent of the evidence.

If you think you know the answer then write it down on your RESEARCH AND THEORY SHEET, giving the reasons. Fill in your name at the top and show it to the facilitator whereupon you cease being a player and become a facilitator's assistant. Thus, you can have one guess only.

The first player to show the right answer and right reason to the facilitator is the winner and scores 100 points, the second player to do so scores 90 points, etc. The first player with the right reason and the wrong answer (or the other way round) scores 50 points, and the next such player scores 40 points, etc.

K. Jones 1992, published by Kogan Page

RELATIVE LETTERS GAME

(cut out)

c	m	m
m	c	m
m	m	c
m	m	m

RELATIVE LETTERS GAME   Clue Cards

(cut out cards)

Clue one: The answer is a number

Clue two: Alphabetic order is irrelevant

Clue three: The question is - What is the value of E?

Clue four: The answer was not known before you started

Clue one: The answer is a number

Clue two: Alphabetic order is irrelevant

Clue three: The question is - What is the value of E?

Clue four: The answer was not known before you started

Clue one: The answer is a number

Clue two: Alphabetic order is irrelevant

Clue three: The question is - What is the value of E?

Clue four: The answer was not known before you started

K. Jones 1992, published by Kogan Page

RELATIVE LETTERS GAME   Research and Theory

Name ....

Player	Evidence	Theory

Small World is a game in which players exchange brief stories of the 'It's a small world' type, and have to guess whether the stories are fact or fiction.

Numbers: The minimum is six or seven. There is no maximum.

Time: A useful guide is to allow a basic ten minutes for thinking and writing down stories plus two or three minutes for each player, up to a limit of about an hour.

Materials: One copy for each player of the STORY SUMMARY SHEET and STORY APPRAISAL FORM.

Procedure: Hand out to each player the PLAYERS' NOTES, STORY SUMMARY SHEET and STORY APPRAISAL FORM. You could emphasize the point that meetings should take place in threes. Arrange for an area of confidentiality, or use such areas as corridors.

Debriefing: Perhaps the starting point can be a brief summary of all the stories, during which the authors state whether they are fact or fiction, enabling the other players to write their scores on the STORY APPRAISAL SHEET. Note that telling a fictional story was not the same as telling lies. Everyone knew that each story was deliberately intended to be either factual or fictional, and the authors simply deferred revealing the category until after the game.

Small World is a game in which players exchange brief stories of the 'It's a small world' type, and have to guess whether the stories are fact or fiction.

First, think of a story of some coincidence and write it down, in not more than 20 words, on the STORY SUMMARY SHEET, adding your name at the end. The story should be either completely true or completely false, not a half truth or a coincidence that nearly happened.

Players meet privately in threes (not in pairs, fours or larger numbers) and introduce themselves. They take it in turn to tell their story briefly (not more than about half a minute each), or show the summary of their story. After each story the other two players are allowed to ask one question each. Each player writes down a title for each story of not more than five words on the STORY APPRAISAL FORM and enters FACT, FICTION or DON'T KNOW. The player telling the story must not reveal whether it is fact or fiction, and the appraisal guesses should not be revealed either.

At the end of the game the players reveal whether their stories were fact or fiction. If the guess is correct then the score is three. If the guess is incorrect then the score is nil. If DON'T KNOW has been entered there is an automatic score of one point.

The player with the highest total score wins.

SMALL WORLD

Story Summary Sheets

(cut out - four cards)

Story summary

_____

_____

_____

Story summary

_____

_____

_____

Story summary

_____

_____

_____

Story summary

_____

_____

_____

Story summary

_____

_____

_____

K. Jones 1992, published by Kogan Page

SMALL WORLD   Story Appraisal Form

Player	Small World Story	Fact	Fiction	Don't know

Takeover is a game in which each player starts as the owner of a company containing one of three words - ACES, KINGS or TWOS. When a company is taken over the staff of that company receive jobs one step lower in the hierarchy.

Numbers:
Probably the minimum number is about 12. Although it will work with smaller numbers the game will not last very long. There is no maximum number.

Time:
Allow ten minutes, plus one minute per player.

Materials:
One copy for each player of the COMPANY OWNERSHIP FORM.

Procedure:
Hand out the PLAYERS' NOTES. Place the COMPANY OWNERSHIP FORMS face down on a table and ask players to pick their own, warning them to conceal the name of their company from other players, otherwise they risk being on the losing end of a takeover. Try to arrange a section of the room where private meetings can take place without too much danger of deliberate or accidental espionage.

Debriefing:
In this game it is fairly obvious who has won, and since there is a minimum amount of skill involved there is probably little point in having a debriefing apart from asking people what they thought of the event as (a) an icebreaker and (b) a game. However, interesting ideas can surface and it is useful to allow time to discuss these.

PLAYERS' NOTES

Takeover is a game in which each player starts as the owner of a company containing one of three words - ACES, KINGS or TWOS. When a company is taken over the staff of that company receive jobs one step lower in the hierarchy.

It is vital not to reveal the name of your company until you have to, otherwise you could be on the losing end of a takeover bid. On receiving your COMPANY OWNERSHIP FORM fold it immediately, retire to a relatively secluded spot and write your full name on the top line to become part of the name of the company, (The Sally Brown Twos Company). Then fill in whatever jobs (in descending order) that you think are appropriate for the last two lines.

The first meeting must always be in pairs at which owners (singles) meet only other single player companies. As companies grow in size they should seek to meet companies smaller than themselves wherever possible. Meetings must be private and must be between two companies only, A company cannot refuse a meeting. After introducing themselves the owners of each company reveal, secretly, the company name on the COMPANY OWNERSHIP FORM. If the two companies are the same type (i.e. two Aces) there is no takeover and the two sides must each seek a meeting with another company. If the companies are of different types then:

> *Kings take over Twos*
> *Twos take over Aces*
> *Aces take over Kings*

The owner (and any staff) of the company taken over writes the name of the new company on the first available line of the COMPANY OWNERSHIP FORM. Thus, an owner taken over becomes a director, a director becomes a manager, and so on. The owner (and any staff) of the successful company write nothing on their forms. The game ends when there is only one company left or when all remaining companies are of the same type. The winner is the surviving owner(s) and the runners up are determined by their position in the hierarchy.

Company Ownership Forms

(Cut out - each card is different)

OWNER OF .... **Aces Company**

DIRECTOR OF .... Company

MANAGER OF .... Company

HEAD OF DEPARTMENT OF .... Company

.... Company

.... Company

OWNER OF .... *Kings Company*

DIRECTOR OF .... Company

MANAGER OF .... Company

HEAD OF DEPARTMENT OF .... Company

.... Company

.... Company

OWNER OF .... Twos Company

DIRECTOR OF .... Company

MANAGER OF .... Company

HEAD OF DEPARTMENT OF .... Company

.... Company

.... Company

K. Jones 1992, published by Kogan Page

Tough Maze is a game in which players each receive a segment of a maze and have to meet in pairs, show each other their segments, and try to work out the whole of the maze. Altogether there are nine segments. They are labelled T-O-U-G-H-M-A-Z-E in random order. Each segment overlaps with two, three or four other segments.

Numbers: The minimum is nine. There is no maximum.

Time: Start with a basic ten minutes then add about one minute for each player.

Materials: A MAZE SEGMENT, MAZE PLOTTER and ENTRY FORM - one for each player.

Procedure: When you cut out the MAZE SEGMENTS make each the same size and avoid adding an extra margin to the outside squares, as this would give the game away. With more than nine players simply cut out new segments since players merge if they have the same segment. Keep the segments together in sets to avoid inadvertent disasters. An absence of segment T is not compensated for by having several O segments. Hand out the PLAYERS' NOTES, MAZE PLOTTER and ENTRY FORM. Then distribute the MAZE SEGMENTS - perhaps by placing them face down on a table and asking the players to pick their own segment.

Debriefing: Find some way of demonstrating the correct answer, perhaps by holding up or passing around the winner's entry. The correct answer is when the nine segments are in this letter order: O T A   and look like:

E M Z

G U H

The debriefing could discuss strategies - did players concentrate on their own segments and try to expand step-by-step or did they copy down other players' segments and see how they might fit? Did they adopt a logical approach and perhaps work out that if they could identify the four corner segments and place them in position this would reveal the complete maze?

Tough Maze is a game in which players each receive a segment of a maze and have to meet in pairs, show each other their segments, and try to work out the whole of the maze. Altogether there are nine segments. They are labelled T-O-U-G-H-M-A-Z-E in random order, each letter being in the top left hand corner of each SEGMENT. Each SEGMENT overlaps with two, three or four other segments. It is important to preserve the secrecy of your own segment, and particularly your MAZE PLOTTER (fold it to preserve your theories).

Players cannot refuse to meet, and each player must reveal the MAZE SEGMENT, and take reasonable precautions against other players catching a glimpse of their SEGMENT and MAZE PLOTTER. It is permissible to meet the same player twice. If you meet a player with an identical segment to your own you merge into one player and must stick together.

All meetings are formal - players must first introduce themselves, then reveal their MAZE SEGMENTS, and then go on to meet someone else. If they spot that their segment will fit the segment of the player they are meeting, they should not reveal this. Nor should they enter into discussion, or make comments on what might fit where. However, immediately after each meeting the two players can separately and privately write down information, theories, or notes on their MAZE PLOTTER.

A few hints: You can think of your segment as consisting of four squares. If you can find two of your squares that overlap accurately with those of another player then this is a guaranteed match. But if only one of your squares overlaps accurately with the square of another player (a corner-corner overlap) it may, or may not be, a correct match. Note that the letter in the top left hand 'square' shows the correct orientation as it relates to the other segments. This means that any 'match' obtained by twisting your SEGMENT so that the letter is upside down, or sideways, to the letter on the other player's SEGMENT guarantees that you have got it wrong.

The winner is the first player to show the correct maze drawn on the ENTRY FORM. If the entry is incorrect then the player ceases to take part in the game and must offer their services to the facilitator.

K. Jones 1992, published by Kogan Page

TOUGH MAZE

(cut out, remembering not to add an extra margin to the outside squares)

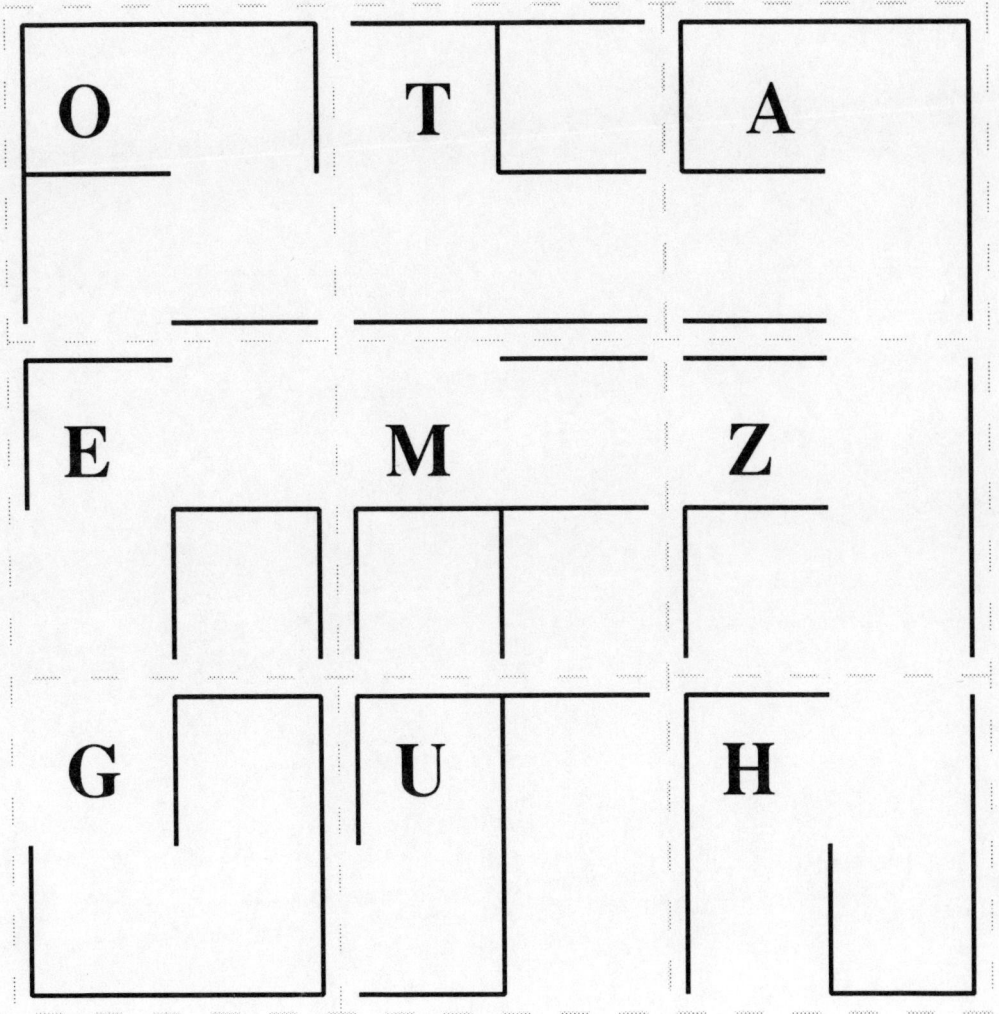

TOUGH MAZE

Do not write anything on this form until you have worked
it all out on the Maze Plotter - there are no second guesses.

K. Jones 1992, published by Kogan Page

Notes and theories:

....

....

....

....

....

Valuegrams is a game in which players try to form a (dictionary) word of not more than six letters in length, each letter taken from a different player's name. There is a preliminary co-operative task to allocate numerical values to most of the letters in each name.

Numbers: The minimum is probably about six. There is no maximum.

Time: Allow about two minutes for each player.

Materials: NAME VALUE CARDS, JOTTINGS SHEET, ENTRY FORM - one copy for each player.

Procedure: Read the PLAYERS' NOTES carefully and make sure you understand how the letters receive their values. In the examples of Ben and Anne in PLAYERS' NOTES the reason only one 'n' receives a number is because there is only one 'n' in 'bean' and the reason for the number 4 is because there are four letters in 'bean'. Hand out the PLAYERS' NOTES, one copy for each player, together with the other three documents - NAME VALUE CARDS (one card each), JOTTINGS SHEET and ENTRY FORM.

Debriefing: Arrange some way in which players can announce their scores - perhaps by taking it in turns to call them out. The winner(s) could be asked to display their lists and this could lead to a discussion of the strategies adopted.

K. Jones 1992, published by Kogan Page

VALUEGRAMS

PLAYERS' NOTES

Valuegrams is a game in which players try to form a (dictionary) word of
not more than six letters in length, each letter taken from a different player's
name. There is a preliminary cooperative task to allocate numerical values to
most of the letters in each name.

For the preliminary task write down the long or short version of your
name on your NAME VALUE CARD. Then meet in pairs and try to find a
word which includes letters from the two names. (You cannot use only your
own name.) The number of letters in the word then becomes the value of each
of the letters and you write these numbers under the appropriate letters of your
name. If Ben met Anne and they decided to make the word 'bean' there are
various options:

  (1) Anne   Ben   (2) Anne   Ben   (3) Anne   Ben
      44 4   4   44   44   4   444

The second option is best because both players would then have completed the
task. Keep meeting other players until at least half your letters have numbers.
Note that there is no advantage in having a high 'score' as players cannot use
their own names in the game itself.

The game begins once the preliminary round is completed, and not
before. Players again meet in pairs to individually form words of six letters or
less, but taking only one letter from any other player's name. You cannot use
your own name. The JOTTINGS SHEET can be used to note numerical values.
If Sara is S-3, a-3, r-0, a-5 and Sam is S-5, a-2, m-0 then a third player could
make a score of ten by forming 'as', using the final 'a' from Sara and the 's'
from Sam. The final word could contain the same letter more than once but
each must be taken from a different player's name.

All meetings must cease two minutes before the end of the game when the
ENTRY FORM must be filled in. The player with the highest numerical score
is the winner, even though the word might have fewer letters than some lower
scoring words of other players.

STOP.

K. Jones 1992, published by Kogan Page   91

(Cut out)

Entry Form

NAME   LETTER VALUE

....

....

....

....

....

TOTAL   ....

Entry Form

NAME   LETTER VALUE

....

....

....

....

....

TOTAL   ....

Entry Form

NAME   LETTER VALUE

....

....

....

....

....

TOTAL   ....

Entry Form

NAME   LETTER VALUE

....

....

....

....

....

TOTAL   ....

VALUEGRAMS   Name Value Cards

Name Value Card

Name Values

Name Value Card

Name Values

Name Value Card

Name Values

Name Value Card

Name Values

Name Value Card

Name Values

Name Value Card

Name Values

Name Value Card

Name Values

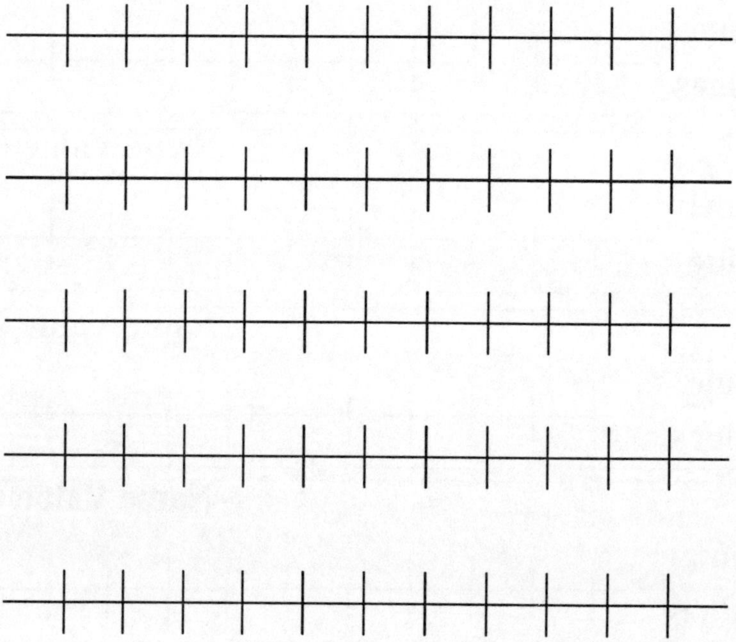

Notes

....

....

....

....

K. Jones 1992, published by Kogan Page

Winning Lines is a game based on the nine-square matrix of Noughts and Crosses (Tic-Tac-Toe).

Numbers: The minimum number of players is probably nine, and there is no maximum. It might be possible to run it with eight, leaving out the centre square.

Time: The game will probably not last for more than ten minutes. It ends when three players have formed themselves into a (legitimate) winning line (horizontal, vertical or diagonal) of all noughts or all crosses.

Materials: Sufficient copies of the SEGMENT SHEET (nine segment cards). With 20 players you will require three SEGMENT SHEETS, and will use two of the nine segments on the third sheet.

Procedure: Hand out the PLAYERS' NOTES. If the numbers are not divisible by nine then use extra cards. The first batch of extra cards can be the four corners, next the four middles of each side, and finally the centre card. Place all cards face down and ask the players to pick their own.

Debriefing: Depending on the participants' interests and the nature of the course, any debriefing could look at the strategies adopted by the players - for example, did they remain single and look at all options, or form into the first pair available and seek a third player?

Winning Lines is a game based on the nine-square matrix of Noughts and Crosses (Tic-Tac-Toe).

Each player is given a SEGMENT CARD with a geometrical shape representing one of the nine shapes (squares) in the matrix. Players must write their name on the line at the bottom of the SEGMENT CARD. The name shows the right way up and allows players to work out which of the nine shapes it is. Players must individually, randomly and secretly choose either a nought or a cross, and then write this symbol boldly in the centre of the shape on their SEGMENT CARD, taking reasonable precautions to prevent other players from seeing their card. Eavesdropping, hovering, or trying to see other players' SEGMENT CARDS from a distance is not permitted

The aim of the game is that players try to form a trio which can make a winning line - all noughts or all crosses in a straight line - vertically, or horizontally, or diagonally.

The first stage is that single players must meet in pairs only (not threes or larger groups) and each player then reveals (in secret) their own SEGMENT CARD. Subsequent stages are a continuation of the first with the following conditions:

1. A pair can split up at any time if either player wishes to do so.
2. Pairs can meet only singles. A single can meet only a single or a pair, and meetings between three singles are not permitted.
3. If a trio is not a winning line it must split into the original single and pair.
4. All meetings must be held in confidence.

The winner is the first trio to achieve a winning line.

K. Jones 1992, published by Kogan Page

WINNING LINES

Segment Sheet

(cut out the nine segments)

Name.........................	Name..........................	Name..........................
Name.........................	Name..........................	Name..........................
Name.........................	Name..........................	Name..........................

5

The exercises

CHARITABLE INTENTIONS   FACILITATOR'S NOTES

Charitable Intentions is an exercise in which pairs design new charities, and seek opinions about their viability.

Numbers: The minimum is about six. There is no maximum.

Time: Allow about two minutes for each participant.

Materials: One copy of the CHARITY DESCRIPTION and VIABILITY RATING for each pair. Clipboards would be useful.

Procedure: Arrange for private areas where participants can devise their charity plus a clear space where participants can collect opinions. Hand out the PARTICIPANTS' NOTES, one copy for each participant. Divide the participants at random into pairs, and hand out to each pair a copy of the CHARITY DESCRIPTION and VIABILITY RATING.

Debriefing: Arrange for some way in which the participants can publicize their findings. This need not take long since most participants will already know what other people have chosen as their charities. The discussion can cover people's motives and intentions, and perhaps make comparisons with existing charities. But bear in mind that this was just an icebreaker exercise, not a sociological study. The discussion is probably more interesting when the emphasis is placed on the process of decision-making rather than the actual decisions themselves. The debriefing could deal with the imagination involved, the logical thoughts, the presentation and communication skills.

CHARITABLE INTENTIONS   PARTICIPANTS' NOTES

Charitable Intentions is an exercise in which pairs design new charities, and seek opinions about their viability.

Most people who are in need of help are already looked after by the well-known charities. Work in pairs and devise a new charity to cover unusual cases - such as the Distressed Husbands' Aid Association. It can be amusing, but should not be too jokey. Think of any class of people who might need help - pedestrians, shoppers, film critics. Decide on the nature of the aid - money, shelter, counselling services, psychiatric help, support groups, providing information, etc.   Enter this on the CHARITY DESCRIPTION form. (If you cannot agree then each do your own charity.)

Now use the VIABILITY RATING to obtain views from other pairs about your invented charity, and reciprocate with your view about the other invented charities. Do not spend much time in discussion or contemplation - a quick response is what is required, even if it is Don't Know.

K. Jones 1992, published by Kogan Page

CHARITABLE INTENTIONS   Charity Description Cards
(Cut out)

Charity Description

Proposer ....

Charity.......................................

....

Aims, etc ....

....

....

....

....

Charity Description

Proposer ....

Charity.......................................

....

Aims, etc ....

....

....

....

Charity Description

Proposer ....

Charity.......................................

....

Aims, etc ....

....

....

....

....

Charity Description

Proposer ....

Charity.......................................

....

Aims, etc ....

....

....

....

CHARITABLE INTENTIONS   Viability Rating

Participants ....

Name of charity ....

Participants   Comments on the charity

K. Jones 1992, published by Kogan Page

COINCIDENCES   FACILITATOR'S NOTES

Coincidences is an exercise in which pairs exchange information about themselves and try to find coincidences. Any coincidence where the probability is estimated at less than one chance in ten (1 in 100, 1,000, 10,000+) is written down.

Numbers: The minimum number is probably about six. There is no maximum.

Time: Allow about two minutes for each participant.

Materials: One copy for each participant of CHECKLIST and PROBABILITY SHEET.

Procedure: Hand out the PARTICIPANTS' NOTES together with the CHECKLIST and PROBABILITY SHEET. You might wish to arrange for two areas, an Introductions Area where people can pair off and a Coincidence Area where they can run through the checklist for coincidences.

Debriefing: Arrange for some procedure whereby participants can announce their findings. With any medium-sized group it will be surprising if no remarkable coincidence emerges. There may be some discussion about the probability level - for example, the chances of meeting someone who went to the same school. (The answer depends on the background of the whole group.) However, remember that the event is an icebreaker, not a sociological survey. The debriefing could also deal with the human interaction - the partnerships, politeness, and effectiveness (or otherwise) of the communication skills.

Coincidences is an exercise in which pairs exchange information about themselves and try to find coincidences. Any coincidence where the probability is estimated as less than one chance in ten (100, 1,000, 10,000+) is written down.

The checklist is merely a guide. You can add to it or amend it.

All meetings are in pairs and you must write down the name of your partner on the PROBABILITY SHEET. Then skim quickly through the CHECKLIST - if no coincidences are found just draw a line though the probability columns on the right. Do not struggle to find coincidences if none are immediately apparent.

The probabilities you are looking for relate to the other participants. So if most participants are engineering students then the probability of meeting another engineering student is too high to be entered. If the pair cannot agree on the coincidence level immediately then toss a coin.

Do not ask for, and do not disclose, any information which could be regarded as an invasion of privacy, such as your age, your income, your religion, your politics or your sex life. Should you be asked such a question then just say something like 'Let's move on to the next item'.

K. Jones 1992, published by Kogan Page

COINCIDENCES

(cut out)

Checklist	Checklist
Birthday Place of birth Education Job Leisure Holidays Family	Birthday Place of birth Education Job Leisure Holidays Family ....
Checklist	**Checklist**
Birthday Place of birth Education Job Leisure Holidays Family	Birthday Place of birth Education Job Leisure Holidays Family ....
Checklist	**Checklist**
Birthday Place of birth Education Job Leisure Holidays Family	Birthday Place of birth Education Job Leisure Holidays Family ....

COINCIDENCES

Probability Sheet

Name ....

Participant	Coincidence	One chance in			
		10	100	1,000	10,000+

K. Jones 1992, published by Kogan Page

Corporate Image is an exercise in which pairs form their own corporation, company or institution, choose three attributes they do not need for the corporate image, and then exchange these attributes with other pairs.

Numbers: The minimum is about six. There is no maximum.

Time: Allow ten minutes, plus about two minutes for each participant.

Materials: One copy for each pair of participants of the CORPORATE IMAGE SHEET and the UNWANTED ATTRIBUTE CARD.

Procedure: Hand out to each participant a copy of the PARTICIPANTS' NOTES and then divide them, preferably at random, into pairs. Hand out to each pair a copy of the CORPORATE IMAGE SHEET and the UNWANTED ATTRIBUTE CARD.

Debriefing: Arrange for some way in which pairs can announce their attributes. This need not take long since many people will already know what attributes others have chosen. The discussion could focus on the concept of the images. Are they useful or counter-productive? Do images give the impression of duplicity or provide a valuable piece of information? As well as looking at the results, the debriefing could deal with the processes - the imagination involved, the logical thoughts, the presentation and communication skills.

Corporate Image is an exercise in which pairs form their own corporation, company or institution, choose three attributes they do not need for the corporate image, and then exchange these attributes with other pairs.

First agree with your colleague on what type your corporation is - a business, a school, the Air Force, a charity, a circus, etc. Write down your names, the name of the organization and the sort of image required at the top of the CORPORATE IMAGE SHEET. The UNWANTED ATTRIBUTE CARD is for three attributes which would have low priority or be absolutely useless to your organization, but which might be fine for other organizations. If your corporation is a detective agency then one of your unwanted attributes could be 'openness'. Try to avoid words like 'good', 'useful', and simply describe the attribute - high technology, artistic, honest, smart, etc. Use not more than three words for each attribute.

When pairs meet they show each other their UNWANTED ATTRIBUTE CARDS. If you want an attribute from another corporation's card you can copy it onto your CORPORATE IMAGE SHEET provided the other pair takes one of your attributes which must be crossed off your UNWANTED ATTRIBUTE CARD and recorded on your CORPORATE IMAGE SHEET. At each meeting only one pair of attributes can be copied from the cards to the sheets.

A second way of acquiring new attributes is by exchanging attributes from the sheets themselves, which allows you to dispose of attributes you have acquired from other pairs and exchange them for ones which seem more suitable. Pairs may exchange as many attributes in this way as they can agree upon. The aim is to meet as many other pairs as possible in order to have the widest choice of attributes.

K. Jones 1992, published by Kogan Page

CORPORATE IMAGE

Corporate Image Sheet

Names ....

Organization ....

Image required ....

ATTRIBUTE	RECEIVED FROM	GIVEN TO

CORPORATE IMAGE   Unwanted Attribute Cards

(cut out)

Unwanted Attributes

Names ....

Organization ....

1 ....

2 ....

3 ....

Unwanted Attributes

Names ....

Organization ....

1 ....

2 ....

3 ....

Unwanted Attributes

Names ....

Organization ....

1 ....

2 ....

3 ....

Unwanted Attributes

Names ....

Organization ....

1 ....

2 ....

3 ....

Unwanted Attributes

Names ....

Organization ....

1 ....

2 ....

3 ....

Unwanted Attributes

Names ....

Organization ....

1 ....

2 ....

3 ....

K. Jones 1992, published by Kogan Page

ENDANGERED SPECIES   FACILITATOR'S NOTES

Endangered Species is an exercise in which participants are given the names of a species (imaginary) and have to invent habitat, appearance and behaviour and then collect comments on the species.

Numbers: The minimum is about five. There is no maximum.

Time: Allow a basic ten minutes for devising habitat, appearance and behaviour plus about two minutes for each participant.

Materials: One copy for each participant of the NAME OF SPECIES, SPECIES DATA CARD and APPRAISAL FORM. Clipboards would be useful.

Procedure: Photocopy the documents and cut out the NAME OF SPECIES CARDS. Hand out to all participants the PARTICIPANTS' NOTES, SPECIES DATA CARDS and APPRAISAL FORM. The NAME OF SPECIES CARDS should be allocated at random, perhaps placed face down on a table and the participants pick their own. The first stage, devising details about a threatened species, should be done singly and in private without consultation. The second stage envisages an area where participants can move around and meet in pairs.

Debriefing: Arrange for some procedure whereby the participants can announce their findings. This can be quite brief since many participants will already know what is on other people's lists. The debriefing could cover such areas as the characteristics of species which appeal to the protective instincts of human beings. It could also cover imagination, humour, politeness, plausibility and communication skills.

ENDANGERED SPECIES   PARTICIPANTS' NOTES

Endangered Species is an exercise in which participants are given the names of a species (imaginary) and have to invent habitat, appearance and behaviour and then collect comments on the species.

You each receive a NAME OF SPECIES CARD. In imagining your species you can add an adjective or two to the name, perhaps using such words or phrases as: black-tailed, Californian, European, lesser, web-footed, etc. Copy the name onto your SPECIES DATA CARD and fill in brief details of habitat, appearance, and behaviour. You should complete this stage yourself, in private.

In obtaining comments you must meet in pairs only. You then show each other your SPECIES DATA CARD. You are not forbidden to exchange extra information about your species, but such exchanges should not take the form of pleas, persuasion or propaganda. You are not allowed to invent extra facts beyond habitat, appearance and behaviour. For example, you cannot claim that the species is being hunted by human beings, or that there are only 350 of the species still in existence. All the species are equally endangered.

Ask each person you meet to write their own name (clearly and in capital letters) in the appropriate column of the APPRAISAL FORM and make whatever comments they like.

K. Jones 1992, published by Kogan Page

ENDANGERED SPECIES   Name of Species

(cut out)

Andime	Borkel	Colvit	Diftig
Elak	Foper	Grisk	Hurlite
Inlope	Juvjuv	Kwilet	Lago
Moirut	Nespeg	Occin	Poffil
Quincel	Rodoro	Squilk	Truke
Uting	Viltagger	Wope	Yesting

ENDANGERED SPECIES

Species Data Cards
(cut out)

Species Data

Name of species ....

Habitat ....

Appearance ....

Behaviour ....

....

Species Data

Name of species ....

Habitat ....

Appearance ....

Behaviour ....

....

Species Data

Name of species ....

Habitat ....

Appearance ....

Behaviour ....

....

K. Jones 1992, published by Kogan Page

ENDANGERED SPECIES   Appraisal form

Participant's name ....

Name of species ....

Name of Appraiser	Comments by Appraiser

Exercise Plan is an exercise in which groups interchange members and take part in the step-by-step design of an exercise.

Numbers: The minimum number is about eight. There is no maximum.

Time: Allow a basic ten minutes, plus one or two minutes for each participant.

Materials: One copy for each pair of the IDEAS FORM and the APPRAISAL FORM. Clipboards could be useful.

Procedure: Photocopy and hand out to each person the PARTICIPANTS' NOTES and divide the participants into pairs, preferably at random, and arrange them in a circle, perhaps with a table for each pair. Then hand out the IDEAS FORM only. Set a time limit for each question to be answered and find some method (threats, promises, appeals to good nature) of getting the Movers to move (clockwise) and not stay chatting while another Mover is waiting to join the Stayer. Hand out the APPRAISAL FORMS to the pairs that exist at the end of the design procedure.

Debriefing: Find some way of allowing the participants to publicize the design and the appraisals. The debriefing can start from the assumption that the method of designing exercises was highly inefficient and discuss ways of improving it. Discussion might also focus on those designs which might be worth following up in other circumstances in the future. As well as looking at the results the debriefing could deal with the processes - the imagination involved, the logical thoughts, the presentation and communication skills.

K. Jones 1992, published by Kogan Page

Exercise Plan is an exercise in which groups interchange members and take part in the step-by-step design of an exercise.

You first meet in pairs to answer the first question (and not any other questions) about the exercise you will be designing. Just write in the title (theme). Decide between you which will be the Mover and which the Stayer. At the end of the time limit set by the facilitator the Movers must take the IDEAS FORM and move clockwise around the circle of groups and join the next Stayer where they answer the second question on the form. Movers must always move promptly, even if the ideas are incomplete or in the process of alteration. Movers must not change their role to Stayers and vice versa. This means that all Movers have the same IDEAS FORM that they started out with.

When all four questions have been completed (three moves will have taken place) you stay in your final pair and receive an APPRAISAL FORM. Then visit other pairs and exchange brief comments on the exercises. Don't spend too long on this or have a detailed discussion. Quick first-impression comments are required.

EXERCISE PLAN   Ideas Forms
(cut out)

EXERCISE PLAN   Ideas Form

1. TITLE? ....

2. ACTION? (what they do) ....

   ....

3. MATERIALS?..

   ....

4. LEARNING? ....

   ....

   ....

EXERCISE PLAN   Ideas Form

1. TITLE? ....

2. ACTION? (what they do) ....

   ....

3. MATERIALS?..

   ....

4. LEARNING? ....

   ....

   ....

   K. Jones 1992, published by Kogan Page

EXERCISE PLAN

Appraisal form

Name of participants ....

APPRAISERS	COMMENTS

Game Plan is an exercise in which groups interchange members and take part in the step-by-step design of a game.

Numbers: The minimum number is about eight. There is no maximum.

Time: Allow a basic ten minutes, plus one or two minutes for each participant.

Materials: One copy for each pair of the IDEAS FORM and the APPRAISAL FORM. Clipboards would be useful.

Procedure: Photocopy and hand out to each person the PARTICIPANTS' NOTES and divide the participants into pairs, preferably at random and arrange them in a circle, perhaps with one table for each pair. Then hand out the IDEAS FORM only. Set a time limit for each question to be answered and find some method (threats, promises, appeals to good nature) of getting the Movers to move (clockwise) and not stay chatting while another Mover is waiting to join the Stayer.   Hand out the APPRAISAL FORMS to the pairs that exist at the end of the design procedure.

Debriefing: Find some way of allowing the participants to publicize the design and the appraisals. The debriefing can start from the assumption that the method of designing games was highly inefficient and discuss ways of improving it. Discussion might also focus on those designs which might be worth following up in other circumstances in the future. As well as looking at the results the debriefing could deal with the processes - the imagination involved, the logical thoughts, the presentation and communication skills.

K. Jones 1992, published by Kogan Page

Game Plan is an exercise in which groups interchange members and take part in the step-by-step design of a game.

You first meet in pairs to answer the first question (and not any other questions) about the game you will be designing. Just write in the title (theme). Decide between you which will be the Mover and which the Stayer. At the end of the time limit set by the facilitator the Movers must take the IDEAS FORM and move clockwise around the circle of groups and join the next Stayer where they answer the second question. Movers must always move promptly, even if the ideas are incomplete or in the process of alteration. Movers must not change their role to Stayers and vice versa. This means that all Movers have the same IDEAS FORM that they started out with.

When all four questions have been completed (three moves will have taken place) you stay in your final pair and receive an APPRAISAL FORM. Then visit other pairs and exchange brief comments on the games. Don't spend too long on this or have a detailed discussion. Quick first-impression comments are required.

GAME PLAN

Ideas forms

(cut out)

GAME PLAN   Ideas Form

1. TITLE? ....
2. ACTION? (including scoring) ....

....

3. MATERIALS?..

....

4. LEARNING? ....

....

....

GAME PLAN   Ideas Form

1. TITLE? ....
2. ACTION? (including scoring) ....

....

3. MATERIALS?..

....

4. LEARNING? ....

....

....

K. Jones 1992, published by Kogan Page

GAME PLAN

Appraisal form

Name of participants ....

APPRAISERS	COMMENTS

Half a Vote is an exercise in which everyone has half a vote. The aim is to combine two halves into one, and decide on a topic and forum for using the vote. Groups grow larger if there is consensus.

Numbers: The minimum number is probably about six. There is no maximum.

Time: Allow about two or three minutes for each participant.

Materials: One copy for each participant of the ISSUES FORM.

Procedure: Hand out one copy to each participant of the PARTICIPANTS' NOTES and the ISSUES FORM. Arrange for conditions of reasonable privacy in which participants can fill in the first line about the issue and the forum. The next stage is the forming of pairs and larger groups. For this stage arrange for negotiation areas, perhaps in the corners of the room, with the centre of the room being an introductions area.

Debriefing: If more than one group remains at the end of the event then arrange for a representative of every group to announce the consensus and any points of agreement or disagreement with other groups. Participants who are still single with half a vote could be given the opportunity of explaining why they did not wish to merge. The subsequent discussion can then focus on the issues themselves or, perhaps more usefully, on the behaviour, persuasive power and organizational abilities of the groups.

K. Jones 1992, published by Kogan Page

Half a Vote is an exercise in which everyone has half a vote. The aim is to combine two halves into one, and decide on a topic and forum for using the vote. Groups grow larger if there is consensus.

Working individually, write your name at the top of the ISSUES FORM. Write in a 'real life' issue that you feel to be reasonably important and upon which you are not a 'don't know' person. Your answer could be general (the environment) or specific (chemical pollution of a local river). Then write the forum of debate - it could be local, national or international. It could be the boardroom of a multi-national company or the annual meeting of the local Arts Society - but it must be a forum in which people normally vote.

You now meet, privately, in pairs, to try to find someone who agrees to combine the half votes (which are ineligible) into a full vote which is eligible. To do this either or both participants may need to change one or both items on the ISSUES FORM as their second choice options. You do not have to join your vote with someone else's, you can remain a single half-vote person for the whole of the exercise if you wish. However, once a pair has been formed it must not break up again, and each participant has the power to veto any merger with another pair. Pairs meet other pairs and try to achieve as much consensus as possible, which means entering new options on the ISSUES FORM. Do not stay more than a minute or two with each pair - if you cannot agree then move on, and if you can agree then you form a new group. Once a larger group has been formed it must always remain together and each member has the power of veto on the question of merging.

(cut out)

HALF A VOTE   Issues Form

Name of participant ....

Original issue ....

.... Forum ....

CHANGES

Colleagues   Details

....

....

....

HALF A VOTE   Issues Form

Name of participant ....

Original issue ....

.... Forum ....

CHANGES

Colleagues   Details

....

....

....

Icebreaker Plan is an exercise in which groups interchange members and take part in the step-by-step design of an icebreaker.

Numbers: The minimum number is about eight. There is no maximum.

Time: Allow a basic ten minutes, plus one or two minutes for each participant.

Materials: One copy for each pair of the IDEAS FORM and the APPRAISAL FORM. Clipboards could be useful.

Procedure: Photocopy and hand out to each person the PARTICIPANTS' NOTES and divide the participants into pairs, preferably at random. Arrange them in a circle, perhaps with a table for each pair, then hand out the IDEAS FORM only. Set a time limit for each question to be answered and find some method (threats, promises, appeals to good nature) of getting the Movers to move (clockwise) and not stay chatting while another Mover is waiting to join the Stayer. Hand out the APPRAISAL FORMS to the pairs that exist at the end of the design procedure.

Debriefing: Find some way of allowing the participants to publicize the design and the appraisals. The debriefing can start from the assumption that the method of designing icebreakers was highly inefficient and discuss ways of improving it. Discussion might also focus on those designs which might be worth following up in other circumstances in the future. As well as looking at the results, the debriefing could deal with the processes - the imagination involved, the logical thoughts, the presentation and communication skills.

Icebreaker Plan is an exercise in which groups interchange members and take part in the step-by-step design of an icebreaker.

You first meet in pairs to answer the first question (and not any other questions) about the icebreaker you will be designing. Decide between you which will be the Mover and which the Stayer. At the end of the time limit set by the facilitator the Movers must take the IDEAS FORM and move clockwise around the circle and join the next Stayer where they answer the second question. Movers must always move promptly, even if the ideas are incomplete or in the process of alteration. Movers must not change their role to Stayers and vice versa. This means that all Movers have the same IDEAS FORM that they started with.

When all four questions have been completed (three moves will have taken place) you stay in your final pair and receive an APPRAISAL FORM. Then visit other pairs and exchange brief comments on the icebreakers. Don't spend too long on this or have a detailed discussion. Quick first-impression comments are required.

K. Jones 1992, published by Kogan Page

ICEBREAKER PLAN   Ideas Forms

(cut out)

ICEBREAKER PLAN   Ideas Form

1. TITLE? ....

2. ACTION? (what they do) ....

....

3. MATERIALS? ....

....

4. LEARNING? ....

....

ICEBREAKER PLAN   Ideas Form

1. TITLE? ....

2. ACTION? (what they do) ....

....

3. MATERIALS? ....

....

4. LEARNING? ....

....

ICEBREAKER PLAN

Appraisal form

Name of participants ....

APPRAISERS	COMMENTS

K. Jones 1992, published by Kogan Page

'Is' in the Middle is an exercise in which the participants devise their own sayings of not more than five words in length from a list of words, with each saying containing 'is' somewhere about the middle. The sayings are shuffled and allocated at random. Participants meet in pairs to try to match sayings with authors.

Numbers: The minimum number is about six and there is no maximum.

Time: Allow ten minutes plus about one or two minutes for each participant.

Materials: One copy for each participant of the RESTRICTED WORD LIST, SAYINGS CARD and SAYINGS LIST.

Procedure: Hand out the PARTICIPANTS' NOTES and the other three documents. Collect the SAYINGS CARDS as they are filled in, shuffle them, and place them face down on a table where they can be collected.

Debriefing: Any debriefing will probably be determined by the circumstances. For example, did participants make guesses about which author wrote which saying, and on what did they base their guess? Although such discussions are usually humorous and enlightening, facilitators should be on the alert for danger signals - people being hurt because of references to themselves, or accusing others of prejudice or stereotyping. Remember that this was an icebreaker exercise involving sayings, not a personality inventory. However, the debriefing could deal with the human interaction - the partnerships, creativity, analysis of problems, politeness, and effectiveness (or otherwise) of the communication skills.

'Is' in the Middle is an exercise in which the participants devise their own sayings of not more than five words in length from a restricted list of words, with each saying containing 'is' somewhere about the middle. The sayings are shuffled and allocated at random. Participants meet in pairs to try to match sayings with authors.

Write your saying in secret (and twice) on your SAYINGS CARD. Do not use words which are not on the RESTRICTED WORD LIST. It is not a condition that you must agree with your own saying. The saying could be nonsense. Both 'Blue is a cat' and 'A cat is blue' are acceptable. Tear off the top copy of your saying which you keep concealed. It is a reminder, and a proof that it is your saying.

Give the bottom half of the SAYINGS CARD to the facilitator who will shuffle the CARDS and allocate them at random. Write your name at the top of your SAYINGS LIST. When you receive your allocated saying write it at the top of the middle column. If, by chance, it is your own saying do not point this out to anyone. Just write it down, without putting in your own name as author until the end of the exercise.

Participants meet in pairs only. You must (a) introduce yourselves, (b) show the SAYINGS CARD, (c) write down the saying shown by the other participant (even though the saying might be your own) on your SAYINGS LIST. You can then pick two (not more than two) sayings from your list and ask whether or not the other participant is the author of either. If you wish you can exchange information and guesses about who might be authors of the sayings.

K. Jones 1992, published by Kogan Page

(cut out)

is
a an the
blue cat cheating child
cleverness dog fairness game
green illusion joke joy
letter losing man mirror
mistake person play real
red sadness sense sleep star
trouble truth
winning woman word work

is
a an the
blue cat cheating child
cleverness dog fairness game
green illusion joke joy
letter losing man mirror
mistake person play real
red sadness sense sleep star
trouble truth
winning woman word work

is
a an the
blue cat cheating child
cleverness dog fairness game
green illusion joke joy
letter losing man mirror
mistake person play real
red sadness sense sleep star
trouble truth
winning woman word work

is
a an the
blue cat cheating child
cleverness dog fairness game
green illusion joke joy
letter losing man mirror
mistake person play real
red sadness sense sleep star
trouble truth
winning woman word work

is
a an the
blue cat cheating child
cleverness dog fairness game
green illusion joke joy
letter losing man mirror
mistake person play real
red sadness sense sleep star
trouble truth
winning woman word work

is
a an the
blue cat cheating child
cleverness dog fairness game
green illusion joke joy
letter losing man mirror
mistake person play real
red sadness sense sleep star
trouble truth
winning woman word work

(cut out)

Name ....

Saying ....

....

. . . (fold, tear, and keep top half) . . . .

Saying: ....

....

Name ....

Saying ....

....

. . . (fold, tear, and keep top half) . . . .

Saying: ....

....

Name ....

Saying ....

....

. . . (fold, tear, and keep top half) . . . .

Saying: ....

....

Name ....

Saying ....

....

. . . (fold, tear, and keep top half) . . . .

Saying: ....

....

K. Jones 1992, published by Kogan Page

'IS' IN THE MIDDLE

Sayings List

Name of participant ....

PARTICIPANT	SAYING	POSSIBLE AUTHOR

Mixed Wedding is an exercise in which the participants have different pieces of information about a wedding. The problem is to find out who the bride, groom, best man and bridesmaid are, what their jobs are, and what they are wearing.

Numbers: The minimum number is eight. There is no maximum.

Time: Allow about two minutes for each participant.

Materials: One copy of the JOTTINGS SHEET for each participant and one copy of the CLUE CARDS SHEET between every eight participants. Cut up the number of CLUE CARDS required, and if there are more than eight participants keep the cards in their sets to avoid muddle. (The puzzle cannot be solved unless all eight cards are available.) With numbers not divisible by eight add extra cards from the next sheet and if two participants find they have the identical card they merge into one participant and stick together.

Procedure: Arrange for adequate space where participants can meet privately in pairs. Hand out a copy of the PARTICIPANTS' NOTES to each participant, plus the JOTTINGS SHEET and a CLUE CARD.

Debriefing: Make arrangements for publicizing the answer which is:

bride	*Anne*	*bus driver*	*white*
groom	*Don*	*nurse*	*blue*
bridesmaid	*Cora*	*surgeon*	*grey*
best man	*Bob*	*typist*	*red*

The discussion could focus on the fact that although gender helped to rule out wedding options (eg Don could not be the bride or bridesmaid) it did not rule out job options, for example, the surgeon could be a woman. The answer can be worked out in stages. Since Anne is the bride wearing white, and neither Cora nor the best man wears blue, then Don must wear blue. The typist wears red and must be Bob because Cora is not the typist and neither Don nor Anne wear red. So Cora must wear grey, and must be the surgeon. As Anne is not the nurse she must be the bus driver and Don must be the nurse.

Mixed Wedding is an exercise in which the participants have different pieces of information about a wedding. The problem is to find out who the bride, groom, best man and bridesmaid are, what their jobs are, and what they are wearing.

You will receive a CLUE CARD, and individual participants should meet in pairs, introduce themselves, show their CLUE CARDS and co-operate in trying to find the answers. If two participants agree that they have made a correct deduction then they can form into a permanent pair. Pairs can become groups of three or more providing all members introduce themselves and agree on the deductions.

The grids on the JOTTINGS SHEET may help in tackling the problem. You can write in ticks or crosses - a tick if two things are linked, a cross if two things are not linked.

If you meet anyone with an identical CLUE CARD you merge together into one participant, and you must stick together.

Bob is not the bus driver

Anne is not the nurse

The person wearing blue is neither Cora nor the best man

The surgeon is wearing a grey suit

The typist is wearing a red jacket

The bridesmaid is not the typist

The bride is wearing a white dress

Don is marrying Anne

K. Jones 1992, published by Kogan Page

	Name	Job	Clothing
Bride			
Groom			
Bridesmaid			
Best Man			

Jottings

New Taxes is an exercise in inventing new taxes which would help to improve the quality of life or improve efficiency in general.

Numbers: The minimum is probably about eight. There is no maximum.

Time: Allow about two minutes for each participant.

Materials: One NEW TAX APPRAISAL SHEET for each pair. Clipboards could be useful.

Procedure: Hand out one copy to each participant of the PARTICIPANTS' NOTES. Divide the participants into pairs, preferably at random, and give each pair a copy of the NEW TAX APPRAISAL SHEET. Arrange for an area where pairs can meet privately.

Debriefing: Arrange for some way of publicizing the comments on the new taxes. The subsequent discussion could cover specific proposals or the nature of the tax system in general. The debriefing could concentrate on the human interaction - friendship, politeness, on the communication skills of explaining, summarizing and decision-making which should take account not only of the final result but of the thoughts and feelings which led up to it.

New Taxes is an exercise in inventing new taxes which would help to improve the quality of life or improve efficiency in general.

Working in pairs decide on ways to improve efficiency, or the quality of life, or both. Then think of taxes which could help bring this about. If you decide that too much time is wasted in meetings then you could devise a tax on the amount of time spent in meetings. Do not make your proposed tax too jokey - it must be an attempt to deal with a real problem. Write your name on the NEW TAX APPRAISAL SHEET plus the name of the new tax and a brief description.

Then visit other pairs and exchange brief comments on each other's new tax proposal, writing down the comments on the appraisal sheets. Don't spend too long on this or have a detailed discussion. Quick first-impression comments are required.

NEW TAXES

New Tax Appraisal Sheet

PROPOSERS OF NEW TAX ....

NAME OF TAX ....

PURPOSE OF TAX ....

....

APPRAISERS	COMMENTS

K. Jones 1992, published by Kogan Page

Ology is an exercise to invent, define and comment on new 'ologies'.

Numbers: The minimum is probably about six. There is no maximum.

Time: Allow one or two minutes for each participant.

Materials: OLOGY APPRAISAL FORM - one for each participant. Clipboards could be useful.

Procedure: Hand out one copy to each participant of PARTICIPANTS' NOTES and the OLOGY APPRAISAL FORM. Arrange for an area in which individual participants (or pairs of participants) can meet privately.

Debriefing: Arrange for a way to publicize the ologies, the definitions and the examples. This need not take too long since most participants will already know what is on other people's sheets. The debriefing could concentrate on the most interesting ologies, or else take a broader look into sociological aspects. However, remember that this was an icebreaker, not a research survey of undesirable features of modern life. As well as looking at the results, the debriefing could deal with the processes - the imagination involved, the logical thoughts, the presentation and communication skills.

Ology is an exercise to invent, define and comment on new 'ologies'. For example, 'Initialology' might be defined as 'An inclination among large organizations to use initials instead of names'.

Participants can work separately, or as pairs. Write your name(s) on the OLOGY APPRAISAL FORM, plus the title of the ology and a definition. Do not make your ology too jokey - it must be an attempt to focus on a real problem.

Then visit other single participants or pairs and exchange brief comments on each other's new ology. Don't spend too long on this or have a detailed discussion. Quick first-impression comments are required. The comments could concentrate on whether or not the ology was a useful category, but feel free to make whatever comments seem appropriate.

K. Jones 1992, published by Kogan Page

OLOGY

Ology Appraisal Form

PROPOSER(S) OF OLOGY ....

NAME OF OLOGY ....

DESCRIPTION OF OLOGY ....

....

APPRAISER(S)	COMMENTS

RELATIVE LETTERS EXERCISE

FACILITATOR'S NOTES

Relative Letters Exercise is an exercise in which participants try to find out not only the answer but also the question. Each participant receives an EVIDENCE CARD containing a single letter and there are four clue cards handed out by the facilitator for each 20 per cent of the evidence collected. There are also two clues (hints) hidden in the PARTICIPANTS' NOTES.

Numbers: The minimum is about six. There is no maximum.

Time: Allow about two minutes for each participant.

Materials: RESEARCH AND THEORY SHEET - one for each participant, CLUE CARDS - one sheet (12 cards) for every three participants, EVIDENCE CARDS - one sheet (twelve cards) for every ten participants. The reason for having more EVIDENCE CARDS than participants is because it is important to have undistributed cards so that the players can assume, if they wish to do so, that other letters, probably including E, are on the undistributed cards.

Procedure: Hand out the PARTICIPANTS' NOTES, RESEARCH AND THEORY SHEETS, and lay face down the EVIDENCE CARDS to be picked up by the participants at random. Keep the CLUE CARDS in appropriate piles to be handed out on request - and check the RESEARCH AND THEORY SHEETS to see that the requisite percentage of evidence has been obtained.

Debriefing: The extra clues in PARTICIPANTS' NOTES are the words 'theory' and 'relative', suggesting that the answer might have something to do with Einstein's Theory of Relativity, which is $E=mc^2$. To find the answer before the exercise ends count up the 'm' and 'c' cards remaining and deduct these two totals from the total numbers of 'm' and 'c' cards before the exercise began. Square the number of 'c' cards distributed to the participants and multiply it by the number of their 'm' cards. With eight participants (say 6 m and 2 c) the answer is two squared (four) multiplied by six which equals 24. If no one had heard of mc^2, or even not heard of the Theory of Relativity, it does not matter, they were just pre-Einstein, and their research and theories can be judged accordingly. The discussion can begin with problem-solving ideas. How did the winner (if there was one) arrive at the solution?

    K. Jones 1992, published by Kogan Page

RELATIVE LETTERS EXERCISE

Relative Letters Exercise is an exercise in which participants try to find out not only the answer but also the question. Each participant receives an EVIDENCE CARD containing a single letter and there are four clue cards handed out by the facilitator for each 20 per cent of the evidence collected. There are also two clues (hints) hidden in these PARTICIPANTS' NOTES.

You meet in pairs, introduce yourselves, and disclose your EVIDENCE CARDS. After that you can either stick together or split up. Single participants or pairs can form into larger groups provided they introduce themselves and that everyone agrees on the merger.

What you write on your RESEARCH AND THEORY SHEET can be disclosed to other participants, or kept confidential.

After you have obtained 20 per cent of the evidence - that is having met 20 per cent of the total number of participants - ask the facilitator for Clue Card 1. On 40 per cent ask for Clue Card 2, on 60 per cent ask for the third card, and ask for the fourth when you have 80 per cent of the evidence.

If you, or your group, think you know the answer then write it down on your RESEARCH AND THEORY SHEET giving the reasons, and show this to the facilitator. Whether your answer is right or wrong you are appointed facilitator's assistant. This means you have one guess only.

K. Jones 1992, published by Kogan Page   149

RELATIVE LETTERS EXERCISE   Evidence Cards
(cut out)

c	m	m
m	c	m
m	m	c
m	m	m

K. Jones 1992, published by Kogan Page

RELATIVE LETTERS EXERCISE

Clue Cards

(Cut out)

Clue one: The answer is a number

Clue two: Alphabetic order is irrelevant

Clue three: The question is - What is the value of E?

Clue four: The answer was not known before you started

Clue one: The answer is a number

Clue two: Alphabetic order is irrelevant

Clue three: The question is - What is the value of E?

Clue four: The answer was not known before you started

Clue one: The answer is a number

Clue two: Alphabetic order is irrelevant

Clue three: The question is - What is the value of E?

Clue four: The answer was not known before you started

RELATIVE LETTERS EXERCISE   Research and Theory

Name of participant ....

Participant	Evidence	Theory

K. Jones 1992, published by Kogan Page

Room is an exercise involving a room. But the problem concerning the room, and a practical solution, must be deduced from the evidence.

Numbers: The minimum number is about eight. It could work with fewer but it would mean that one or two participants had two INFORMATION CARDS. There is no maximum.

Time: Allow about two minutes for each participant.

Materials: One copy of the sheet containing the INFORMATION CARDS for each eight participants. The individual cards will need to be cut out.

Procedure: If there are more than eight participants then keep each cut-out set of cards together to avoid the danger of handing out too many copies of one card and too few of another. If, with large numbers, two or more participants find they have the same card they merge into one and stick together. Arrange the furniture so that the participants can move freely.

Debriefing: The implicit question is how to escape from a locked room and there is no one correct answer although there are several wrong answers. As the key is made of brass it will not be attracted to the magnet. Possibly the umbrella could be opened outside the window and something thrown at the key to knock it into the umbrella. Perhaps a better way would be to construct a chain of paper clips with a hook at one end and use the umbrella as a fishing rod. The hook in the wall might be unscrewed and screwed into the end of the umbrella. As well as looking at the results, the debriefing could deal with the processes - the imagination involved, the logical thoughts, the presentation and communication skills.

Room is an exercise involving a room. But the problem, and a practical solution, must be deduced from the evidence.

At the start you move about and meet in pairs, not in larger groups. Introduce yourselves, and describe what you know or simply show the INFORMATION CARD to the other person. However, if you agree on a theory or plan you can, if you wish, become a permanent pair.

If you meet someone with the same card as your own then you merge into one and stick together as a single problem-solver.

Groups of three or larger can be formed provided all members introduce themselves, all agree on a likely hypothesis and plan, and all agree to the merger. (Each individual has a right of veto.)   However, this initial agreement need not stop participants coming up with new ideas, or stop groups splitting up if someone diverges from the general consensus.

K. Jones 1992, published by Kogan Page

(cut out)

A

The brass key to the door is on the ledge outside the window but we cannot reach it because the bars on the window are too close for us to get our arms through.

B

The handle of the brass key is sticking out over the ledge outside the window but the bars are too close for us to get our arms through.

C

The door is heavy steel. A metal hook has been screwed in to the wooden frame of the door but there is nothing on the hook.

D

In the drawer of the desk is a tin box with a lot of elastic bands inside. There is also a strong magnet in the drawer.

E

On the desk is a plastic container with pens. There is also a full bottle of glue, and three boxes of paper clips.

F

On the floor in the corner is a hatstand containing a long white coat and an umbrella.

G

On the shelf is a small pair of scissors. There is also a brush and comb, and a small mirror.

H

In the cupboard there is a wire tray, two rolls of toilet paper, and a large bar of soap.

Simulation Plan is an exercise in which groups interchange members and take part in the step-by-step design of a simulation.

Numbers: The minimum number is about eight. There is no maximum.

Time: Allow a basic ten minutes, plus one or two minutes for each participant.

Materials: One copy for each pair of the IDEAS FORM and the APPRAISAL FORM. Clipboards could be useful.

Procedure: Photocopy and hand out to each person the PARTICIPANTS' NOTES and divide the participants into pairs, preferably at random. Arrange them in a circle, perhaps with a table for each pair, then hand out the IDEAS FORM only. Set a time limit for each question to be answered and find some method (threats, promises, appeals to good nature) of getting the Movers to move (clockwise) and not stay chatting while another Mover is waiting to join the Stayer. Hand out the APPRAISAL FORMS to the pairs that exist at the end of the design procedure.

Debriefing: Find some way of allowing the participants to publicize the design and the appraisals. The debriefing can start from the assumption that the method of designing simulations was inefficient and discuss ways of improving it. Discussion might also focus on those designs which might be worth following up in other circumstances in the future. As well as looking at the results, the debriefing could deal with the processes - the imagination involved, the logical thoughts, the presentation and communication skills.

Simulation Plan is an exercise in which groups interchange members and take part in the step-by-step design of a simulation.

You first meet in pairs to answer the first question (and not any other questions) about the simulation you will be designing. Decide between you who will be the Mover and who the Stayer. At the end of the time limit set by the facilitator the Movers must take the IDEAS FORM and move clockwise around the circle and join the next Stayer where they answer the second question. Movers must always move promptly, even if the ideas are incomplete or in the process of alteration. Movers must not change their role to Stayers and vice versa. This means that all Movers have the same IDEAS FORM that they started out with.

When all four questions have been completed (three moves will have taken place) you stay in your final pair and receive an APPRAISAL FORM. Then visit other pairs and exchange brief comments on the simulations. Don't spend too long on this or have a detailed discussion. Quick first-impression comments are required.

SIMULATION PLAN   Ideas forms

(cut out)

SIMULATION PLAN   Ideas Form

1. TITLE? ....

2. ACTION? (including roles) ....

....

3. MATERIALS? ....

....

4. LEARNING? ....

....

SIMULATION PLAN   Ideas Form

1. TITLE? ....

2. ACTION? (including roles) ....

....

3. MATERIALS? ....

....

4. LEARNING? ....

....

K. Jones 1992, published by Kogan Page

SIMULATION PLAN

Appraisal form

Name of participants ....

APPRAISERS	COMMENTS

Starting Again is an exercise about options at birth - the choice being a trade-off between natural ability and parental income.

Numbers: The minimum number is about six. There is no maximum.

Time: Allow about two minutes for each participant.

Materials: One copy for each participant of the OPINIONS SHEET. Clipboards could be useful.

Procedure: Hand out to each participant one copy of the PARTICIPANTS' NOTES plus one copy of the OPINIONS SHEET. Arrange for an area where participants can meet in private.

Debriefing: Arrange for some method whereby participants can announce their findings. This need not take very long since most participants will know a good deal of what is on other people's OPINIONS SHEETS. The discussion can start by asking participants whether their own views differ from those of the mass of the population. As well as looking at the results, the debriefing could deal with the processes - the imagination involved, the logical thoughts, the presentation and communication skills.

Starting Again is an exercise about options at birth - the choice being a trade-off between natural ability and parents' income.

You must make a guess about how you think most people in the country would answer the following question about whether, if they were born again, they would choose to be poor but talented, or have just above average ability but be relatively wealthy. You are also asked to guess the reason most people would have for making that particular choice.

If you had to be born again, which of these three situations would you choose and why?
  a. Your natural ability at the 80% level, parents' income at the 10% level
  b. Your natural ability at the 70% level, parents' income at the 50% level
  c. Your natural ability at the 60% level, parents' income at the 90% level

You can ignore the people who might say they don't know. Your answer must be a, or b, or c and you cannot say 'don't know' because you are not asked for facts, you are asked to make a guess. If you cannot decide between a, b or c then pick one at random and think of a reason why people might choose that option.   You are not being asked for your own views on the question.

The percentages relate to the population as a whole - thus the 80 per cent level means that the person has more natural ability than the bottom 79 per cent but less than the top 19 per cent. 'Natural ability' is a broad concept and is not confined to intelligence. When you have written your guess (and reason) meet in pairs (not trios or larger groups) and introduce yourselves. Fill in other participants' guesses on your OPINIONS SHEET.

If you are in agreement about the guess, and if you agree broadly about the reasons, then you can join together if you wish to do so. Pairs can become larger groups by mutual consent provided (a) everyone introduces themselves, (b) the guess is the same, and (c) the reasons are broadly similar. Groups can also split up if members change their views.   The aim is not to find an 'answer': it is to explore the question.

STARTING AGAIN   Opinions Sheet

NAME ....

My guess is that most people would answer (A or B or C)

Because ....

Guess changed later because ....

....

Participant(s)	Guess	Reasons

K. Jones 1992, published by Kogan Page

Uniqueness is an exercise in the unusual. Each participant writes down something unique about themselves. These cards are then shuffled and handed out and participants try to compile a matching list.

Numbers: The minimum number is about six. There is no maximum.

Time: About two minutes for each participant.

Materials: One copy for each participant of the UNIQUE FEATURES CARD and the FEATURES LIST.

Procedure: Hand out to each participant one copy of the PARTICIPANTS' NOTES and the UNIQUE FEATURES CARD. When the unique features have been handed in, shuffle the cards face down on a table and let the participants pick their own. You can hand out the FEATURES LIST at the same time.

Debriefing: Arrange for some way of announcing the findings - perhaps by people taking it in turn. The discussion could then look for patterns or trends, but remember that the aim was an icebreaker, not a probe of personalities. The debriefing could also consider the human interaction - politeness, understanding, sympathy, shrewdness and communication skills.

Uniqueness is an exercise in the unusual. Each participant writes down something unique about themselves. These cards are then shuffled and handed out and participants try to compile a matching list.

The uniqueness can be important or trivial. Here are some examples:

> I think I am the only person present -
>> *to collect beer mats*
>> *to have written a paper on motorcycle maintenance*
>> *to have met a pop star*
>> *to have never watched a complete episode of a soap opera*
>> *to believe that a woman's place is in the kitchen.*

Write the example on the UNIQUE FEATURES CARD and hand it to the facilitator who will shuffle them; you then take one at random.

When you receive your card write the unique feature on your UNIQUE FEATURES LIST. If it happens to be your own feature you still write it down but do not, at this stage, write in your own name as the author. The first box in the first column is left blank because that feature is received from the facilitator and not shown to you by a participant.

Meet other participants in pairs only, not threes, and write down their names in the first column, and the feature (or a summary of it) in the second column. You can then select one or two (but not more than two) features from your list and ask the person you are meeting if the features belong to them. You can use the third column for accurate information, or for guesses, or both.

Whether you show each other your lists is up to you. It makes the exercise easier if you show it, but perhaps the activity is more intriguing if you do not reveal what you have learned.

K. Jones 1992, published by Kogan Page

UNIQUENESS

Unique Features List

Name of participant ....

Participant	Unique feature	Belongs to

UNIQUENESS

Unique Features Cards
(cut out)

My unique feature is ....

....

My unique feature is ....

....

My unique feature is ....

....

My unique feature is ....

....

My unique feature is ....

....

My unique feature is ....

....

My unique feature is ....

....

K. Jones 1992, published by Kogan Page

Working Slogans is an exercise in which pairs invent an organization and choose a sensible slogan, but the slogan is implemented by others.

Numbers: The minimum is probably about six. There is no maximum.

Time: Allow two or three minutes for each participant.

Materials: SLOGAN SHEET - one copy for each pair.

Procedure: Hand out the PARTICIPANTS' NOTES, one to each participant, and divide the participants into pairs, preferably at random. Hand out one SLOGAN SHEET to each pair. Set a deadline for completion of the SLOGAN SHEET (otherwise some pairs will spend all day on it) then shuffle the sheets and let pairs pick at random. Each pair writes down (briefly) how they would implement the slogan and then takes the sheet round to other pairs and asks for their suggestions, which are also written down.

Debriefing: At the end of the exercise arrange for some way of publicizing some or all of the entries. This need not take too long since most participants will already have seen other participants' work. The discussion could centre on the the way similar situations arise in real life. As well as looking at the results, the debriefing could deal with the processes - the imagination involved, the logical thoughts, the presentation and communication skills.

Working Slogans is an exercise in which pairs invent an organization and choose a sensible slogan, but the slogan is implemented by others.

In the first stage everyone meets as pairs with the job of deciding on an organization, and devising an internal slogan aimed at the staff or a public slogan aimed at the customers/clients. It can be any sort of organization - a multinational company, a newspaper, the Army, a cinema chain - but it must be reasonably large.   Write down the name of the organization and the slogan on your SLOGAN SHEET.

In the second stage you take your SLOGAN SHEETS round to other participants, meeting in fours, and the aim is to imagine how somewhat disenchanted subordinates might implement the slogan. You write down your answer on other people's SLOGAN SHEETS in not more than about ten words.

Implementation ideas should be (a) plausible and (b) mildly subversive. For example, if the public slogan of a supermarket was 'We aim to please' then it would be more plausible to hand each customer a long questionnaire about their needs just before they check out rather than give each customer a free television set. A quick decision is needed. If you cannot think of anything appropriate then don't write anything, or write 'Don't know', and move quickly on to the next meeting.

WORKING SLOGANS   Slogan Sheet

Participants ....

Name and type of organization ....

....

Slogan ....

Aimed at: Staff [ ]   Customers [ ]   Both [ ]

Participants	How the slogan could be implemented

6

The simulations

Artifacts is a simulation set in the distant future where a virus in the computer network has destroyed all records and a group of sociologists, historians and scientists try to find the use for some ancient artifacts known as coin, key, pen, etc.

Numbers: The minimum is probably six. There is no maximum.

Time: Allow about two minutes for each participant.

Materials: Collect some common everyday objects - pen, paperclip, ruler, dice, playing card, chess piece, credit card, soap, etc - about ten should be sufficient. One copy of the DESCRIPTION AND THEORY PAPER for each participant.

Procedure: Hand out to each participant one copy of the PARTICIPANTS' NOTES, and collect these again before the action starts since they do not exist within the event. Divide the participants into groups, preferably at random, and hand out the DESCRIPTION AND THEORY PAPER. With ten participants there could be five groups of two. With 50 participants there could be ten groups of five. Give each group an artifact. Arrange for some area where groups can make their presentations. They could be sitting behind a table, or standing on a rostrum, or any other arrangement which is available and plausible. Fix the time limit for each presentation, or else ask for volunteers for the job of Artifact Research Organizers who can be given the job of working out the mechanics of the event.

Debriefing: Any discussion could cover whatever is appropriate to the course itself - communication, imagination, friendship, co-operation.

Artifacts is a simulation set in the distant future where a virus in the computer network has destroyed all records and a group of sociologists, historians and scientists try to find the use for some ancient artifacts known as coin, key, pen, etc.

You are all members of the Artifacts Research Guild and the occasion is a presentation of theories by various groups of members about the origin and use of certain artifacts. Although some of the artifacts may have an inscription written on them it is in some ancient script which is completely indecipherable.

You first meet in your groups, introduce yourselves, and write down a description of the artifact on your DESCRIPTION AND THEORY PAPER. You can now guess, individually or collectively, what the object was, how it was used, and who used it. If you cannot reach a consensus then the professors holding a minority view will have to indicate this in the formal presentations later. Meanwhile, and in the tradition of ARG co-operation, you are encouraged to visit other groups, particularly if you are in difficulties or if you feel you want to help. However, it is a rule of the ARG that you must (a) introduce yourselves, and (b) be open and forthcoming about your hypotheses. In the ARG it is impolite, not smart, to conceal your views.

In the formal presentations each member of each group must speak and give their (real) name prefixed by the title Professor. In referring to other people's names always say 'Professor So-and-so'. It is important to observe the time limit. Aspects of each presentation should be divided equally between members of the group, and the time should also be divided equally, as befits the ARG doctrine of equality of opportunity and esteem for friendship and fairness. It would be discourteous to the Guild if professors holding minority views tried to take more than their fair share of time.

K. Jones 1992, published by Kogan Page

ARTIFACTS RESEARCH GUILD

Description and Theory Paper

Description
(size, shape, texture, etc)

Theory
(practical, ornamental, religious, etc)

Significance
(sociology, history, education, etc)

Artistic Shapes is a simulation in which participants alternate between being (a) wall mural designers and (b) specialists in drawing ovals or rectangles. The mural designers direct the specialists in drawing the required shapes.

Numbers: The minimum number is probably about six. The maximum number is limited only by the space available.

Time: Allow about two or three minutes for each participant.

Materials: Coloured pens - three or four different colours should be sufficient. MURAL COMPANY CARD, MURAL DESIGN SHEET - one copy for each participant. SPECIALITY CARD - about four cards for every three participants.

Procedure: Hand out the PARTICIPANTS' NOTES, the MURAL DESIGN SHEET, MURAL COMPANY CARDS and SPECIALITY CARDS. Keep some spare SPECIALITY CARDS because some participants may wish to change their speciality during the course of the action. You can, if you wish, divide the space into two parts, a smallish Introductions Area and a larger Work Area. Participants would then meet in the former and move to the larger area for the drawing work. Before starting the event collect all copies of the PARTICIPANTS' NOTES since these are not part of the simulation itself.

Debriefing: Arrange for some presentation area where the mural companies can display, and perhaps explain, their artistic work. This can be done quite briefly, even with large numbers, since most participants will already have seen most of the works. Discussions could cover such topics as relationships between artists and clients.

K. Jones 1992, published by Kogan Page

ARTISTIC SHAPES   NOTES FOR PARTICIPANTS

Artistic Shapes is a simulation in which participants alternate between being (a) wall mural designers and (b) specialists in drawing ovals or rectangles, but not both. The mural designers direct the specialists in drawing the required shapes.

Write your name on your SPECIALITY CARD and the speciality of your choice - oval or rectangle. You can change specialities later if the other option is in greater demand, in which case get a new card from the Facilitator.

Write your name on your MURAL COMPANY CARD so that it reads like a company. You can add a descriptive word or two - Sally's Hi Tech Mural Company, etc. Write your name on your MURAL DESIGN SHEET.

Meetings must take place in pairs only, never threes or larger. Only one mural must be done at each meeting - you do not change roles in the middle of a meeting. At the first meeting you mutually agree who does what, but at all subsequent meetings you must alternate your job. You must never meet the same person twice.

Mural companies must instruct the specialists where to place one oval or one rectangle on the page and what size and colour it should be. After drawing in the (single) shape the specialist should sign it and the meeting is then complete.

Speciality and Company Cards
(cut out)

SPECIALITY CARD *NAME:* *SPECIALITY:*	**MURAL COMPANY CARD** **NAME:**
SPECIALITY CARD *NAME:* *SPECIALITY:*	**MURAL COMPANY CARD** **NAME:**
SPECIALITY CARD *NAME:* *SPECIALITY:*	**MURAL COMPANY CARD** **NAME:**
SPECIALITY CARD *NAME:* *SPECIALITY:*	

K. Jones 1992, published by Kogan Page

Mural Design Sheet

.... **COMPANY**

Boring Skills is a simulation about recruitment to an agency which has been required to provide skilled personnel for a luxury round-the-world cruise. The particular skill required is to be an effective bore.

Numbers: The minimum is probably twelve, but it might work with less. There is no maximum.

Time: Allow about two minutes for each participant.

Materials: USER-FRIENDLY ORGANIZATION MEMO plus APPRAISAL FORM - one copy of each for each pair. Clipboards could be useful, perhaps one for each pair. There are also six THREE-SUBJECTS CARDS each containing three different subjects. Provide one card for each pair.

Procedure: Provide space and arrange furniture so that participants can first meet in pairs, and then in groups of four. A table could be in the centre, but is not essential. Hand out the PARTICIPANTS' NOTES and collect these again before the action begins since they are not part of the event itself. Hand out the USER-FRIENDLY ORGANIZATION MEMO and the APPRAISAL FORM - one copy for each pair. Each pair should be given, at random, one of the six THREE-SUBJECTS CARDS. Set a deadline for each appraisal group session.

Debriefing: Arrange for some methods whereby participants learn of the results - perhaps by each group in turn indicating what happened during the event. This should be a description rather than simply announcing a 'result'. It is probably not appropriate to have any discussion about people's personalities - remember that this was treated as an icebreaking simulation, not a real-life personality assessment.

Boring Skills is a simulation about recruitment to an agency which has been required to provide skilled personnel for a luxury round-the-world cruise. The particular skill required is to be an effective bore.

You are all people who applied for an advertisement by the User-Friendly Organization for staff who can go on the cruise. You all like the idea, find the salary offered more than generous, and hope to get the job - although you are not sure what it entails in practice. As far as the organization is concerned it is satisfied with your qualifications and merely wishes to appraise your skills, including your skills of appraisal since some people may be recruited mainly for their ability to appraise a situation.

You work in pairs and have short meetings with other pairs. After each meeting you briefly and privately assesss the skills of the other pair using an APPRAISAL FORM. The procedure is described in the USER-FRIENDLY ORGANIZATION MEMO. You will also receive a THREE-SUBJECTS CARD. There are six of these cards altogether, each containing three different subjects. The card is shown to the other pair who have to speak boringly to each other on one of the three subjects.

User-Friendly Organization

MEMO

To: Applicants for the position of
            LUXURY CRUISE PERSONNEL

Our clients, the shipping company, have a special
problem with round-the-world cruises. Virtually all
the passengers are rich, most are friendly, some are
complainers, and a small minority are incredibly
selfish. These selfish passengers demand, or even
seize, the best places on the sun lounges, the best
tables in the dining room, the best seats at the
entertainments and on-shore transport. They ignore
polite requests from the cruise personnel. Any
attempts to persuade them to be unselfish turns them
into complainers of the worse sort.

Our clients propose, as an experiment, to recruit
personnel who appear to be passengers, but who attach
themselves to the 'problem passengers' to distract,
deter, and slow them down, without giving offence. We
believe this can be done by employing people as
skilled bores - to talk (avidly?) in a repetitious,
trivial, or dull manner.

You work in a partnership of two and demonstrate
your boring skills to a second pair, and then move on
to form another group of four. Each partnership has a
'Three-subjects card' which they show to the other
pair and ask them to pick a subject and speak boringly
on it. The two speakers assume that they are both
bores, and talk to each other for an equal amount of
time - about 30 seconds each. After both pairs have
displayed their skills, split up, assess, and then
form new groups of four and continue as before. We may
recruit good assessors as well as good bores.

Good luck.

          K. Jones 1992, published by Kogan Page

BORING SKILLS

Three-Subjects Cards

(Cut out. Note that each card is different)

THREE-SUBJECTS CARD **Bore, for one minute, on one of these three subjects** **Babies** **Cars** **Diets**	*THREE-SUBJECTS CARD* **Bore, for one minute, on one of these three subjects** **Clothes** **Health** **Money**
THREE-SUBJECTS CARD **Bore, for one minute, on one of these three subjects** **Gardening** **Psychiatrists** **Television**	*THREE-SUBJECTS CARD* **Bore, for one minute, on one of these three subjects** **Children** **Friends** **Sports**
THREE-SUBJECTS CARD **Bore, for one minute, on one of these three subjects** **Cooking** **Education** **Muddle**	*THREE-SUBJECTS CARD* **Bore, for one minute, on one of these three subjects** **Hobbies** **Jewellery** **People**

User-Friendly Organization

NAMES: ....

FILL IN THIS FORM AS A PAIR <u>AFTER</u> EACH MEETING WITH
ANOTHER PAIR.
Remember that the aim of the borer is to appear to be
very interested in the subject. Boring (as distinct
from boredom) is an active concept.

<u>BORERS</u>   <u>APPRAISAL</u>

K. Jones 1992, published by Kogan Page

Captions is a simulation concerning the annual convention of RAPS (Reporters, Authors and Photographers Society) where delegates are keen to photograph each other and write captions for their pictures which they hope will be included in *Rapture*, the journal of the society.

Numbers: The minimum number is about six. There is no maximum.

Time: Allow about two minutes for each participant.

Materials: One copy of RAPTUROUS NOTES for each participant. One copy for each participant of the LAYOUT SHEET, and it is probably a good idea to run off some extra copies. There are opportunities for social facilities - cups of coffee, etc. A bulletin board for 'publication' of the submitted entries to the journal could be useful.

Procedure: The venue is supposed to be an informal gathering of a society and so it is useful to clear any furniture from the central areas. Hand out one copy each of the PARTICIPANTS' NOTES. When they have been read, retrieve them otherwise they are incongruous. Hand out RAPTUROUS NOTES and the LAYOUT SHEET, perhaps temporarily taking on the role of editor of *Rapture,* or allocating that role (at random) to one or two participants. Spare copies of the LAYOUT SHEET could be left on a table. Make some arrangements, perhaps a news bulletin board, so that participants can see each other's photographs and captions.

Debriefing: The discussion could cover issues concerned with journalism - a news sense, eye-grabbing captions, publicity, invasion of privacy, libel, etc.

Captions is a simulation concerning the annual convention of RAPS (Reporters, Authors and Photographers Society) where delegates are keen to photograph each other and write captions for their pictures which they hope will be included in *Rapture*, the journal of the society.

You can assume that all members are capable of being reporters, authors and photographers. When you see an interesting-looking person or group then you can take a photograph. (Say 'Snap', 'Click', 'Smile please' or whatever.) Then introduce yourself and take the names of the people you have photographed. Retire gracefully and produce a (very) rough sketch of what the picture will look like on the page. Add a caption underneath. A headline above the picture is optional. Take as many photographs as you wish, and allow others to take your photograph.

Mix and mingle, making a point of introducing yourselves. You do not have to take photographs all the time. Do not stay with the same person for more than a few minutes.

K. Jones 1992, published by Kogan Page

RAPTUROUS NOTES

RAP's increasingly popular annual event, the national convention, starts today. The theme of the convention is the merging of the different jobs of reporter, author and photographer. Modern technology, desk top publishing, and many other developments are uniting the three sections of our Society. We not only have common interests, we often have similar work practices. Also, fact is merging with fiction - we can see this in television and in newspapers.

However, to avoid the misunderstandings of our last convention we urge would-be contributors to this journal to beware of making libellous remarks about fellow members, or about anyone else for that matter.

Don't get me wrong. Part of the convention write-up can be a fun event. I'm all for jokes, I love puns. Wickedly funny captions are great. A short quote from colleagues can make a good story.

So, in order to help contributors, I am including in this issue a LAYOUT FORM - just as a guide so that I can see at a glance what your contributions might look like on the page.

Have fun, meet people, learn something useful.

YOUR EDITOR

Rapture - draft layout sheet - add your own stories

Name ....

....

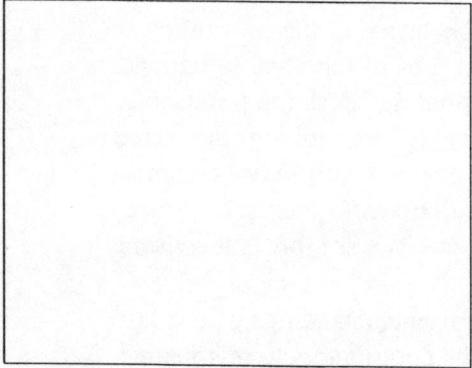

....

....

K. Jones 1992, published by Kogan Page

Designing Countries is a simulation in which the participants work in groups to design their own countries and welcome visitors.

Numbers: Probably the minimum number is six. There is no maximum.

Time: Allow about two or three minutes for each participant.

Materials: One or two copies for each country of the NOTICE OF LAWS, ADVICE TO VISITORS and IMPRESSION. Facilities might include soft drinks. Beware of having armchairs as they have a tendency to block channels. Photocopying facilities could be used for circulating the ADVICE TO VISITORS forms after being filled in by the countries but before the visits take place.

Procedure: Hand out the PARTICIPANTS' NOTES, one copy for each participant, but retrieve all the copies before the event begins. Divide the participants at random into groups. With six there could be three groups of two, with sixty there might be ten groups of six. Hand out the NOTICE OF LAWS, the ADVICE TO VISITORS and IMPRESSION. Set a time limit for designing the countries, otherwise visitors from other countries could find themselves turned away or ignored.

Debriefing: Most countries will already be known to the participants, so the debriefing could start with the waste paper basket - the rejected ideas. The process of design is usually more interesting than the final result. Avoid getting into the 'Our country is best' argument and be wary of emotional and personal criticisms ('You were just a dictator'). The simulation was an icebreaker, not a personality test.

Designing Countries is a simulation in which the participants work in groups to design their own countries and welcome visitors.

The NOTICE OF LAWS is for you to write down any unusual laws. The ADVICE TO VISITORS sheet is to record any sort of information that might be useful - climate, ways of life, etc. You keep IMPRESSION in the visitors' departure lounge so that they can sign their names and add their comments, if any, as they leave.

Do not take too long designing your country - the general picture plus one or two details is all that is required, and you can polish up the image as the visitors arrive and depart. Take it in turn to visit all the other countries. Officials of the host country and the visitors should introduce themselves.

The only firm rule about designing the countries is that visitors must always be welcome.

K. Jones 1992, published by Kogan Page

NOTICE OF LAWS

....

ADVICE TO VISITORS

In order to help visitors enjoy their visit we suggest:

K. Jones 1992, published by Kogan Page

IMPRESSION

We hope that you enjoyed your visit and will come and see us again. Please write in your general impression.

Visitor	Impression

Detective Story is a simulation in which the participants are ideas for characters in an unwritten detective story in the mind of a famous author who has a mental block. The block prevents the ideas from joining together as a group. Participants meet in pairs to try to get the story moving again.

Numbers: The minimum is about eight although it might work with less by omitting a card, or giving two cards to one participant. There is no maximum.

Materials: One copy for each participant of IDEAS SHEET (cloudy shapes). One sheet of CHARACTER CARDS for every eight participants. Keep each set together, as with numbers larger than eight there is a danger of having too many of one card and too few (or none) of another. Note that if two people meet and have an identical card they merge into the same idea and must stick together.

Procedure: Hand out the Participants' Notes to all the participants and retrieve the document before the action begins. Hand out the IDEAS SHEET. The CHARACTER CARDS can be placed face down and the participants can pick their own. Arrange the room like a brain (a classroom with rows of desks perhaps) with lots of pathways intersecting and diverging.

Debriefing: Make arrangements for participants to announce their initiatives. The discussion could cover the question of how the participants co-operated and sent messages to each other. Did they use any procedure for collecting information and co-ordinating ideas?

Detective Story is a simulation in which the participants are ideas for characters in an unwritten detective story in the mind of a famous author who has a mental block. The block prevents the ideas from joining together as a group. Participants meet in pairs to try to get the story moving again.

You will receive, at random, a CHARACTER CARD, which gives you the name of the character together with something they said. There is no information about who your character was speaking to, or the circumstances, or whether the statement was true or false. Show the card to each participant you meet as you circulate around the brain. You will also receive an IDEAS SHEET.

At the start meet only in pairs and make each meeting extremely brief. The writer's block does not permit threes or larger groups except if you come across someone with the same CHARACTER CARD as your own - and you then become the same idea, and stick together like linked neurons.

Later, when you have met at least half of the other ideas, you can start to form into pairs if you find you are thinking on similar lines. The pairs can grow into trios and larger groups. Use the IDEAS SHEET to record information, propose a story line, and make amendments. It shows your development as an idea, and like all ideas you can grow, marry and create. The IDEAS SHEET is not confidential - reveal it to the other ideas you meet.

You are not looking for a story that is there. Your author did not think of a story and then forget it. Your author created a few characters and snippets of dialogue for a detective story but had a mental block before deciding who did what and which were the red herrings. Thus, you are an unemployed idea. You want work and you want to develop. The more agreement there is on a story line the more chance there is of nudging your author back into creativity. In this way you can achieve a purposeful and memorable life.

DETECTIVE STORY

Character Cards

(cut out)

Aunt

And I shall have no hesitation in striking you out of my will.

Butler

I shall endeavour not to mention it.

Lady Eve

My husband, as you must be fully aware, is a gambler.

Lord Adam

I would have you know that I am faithful to my wife.

Maid

One day this could be mine.

Detective

What made you think it was a forgery?

Smith

We want to buy the estate and turn it into a theme park.

Son

I am not on drugs.

 K. Jones 1992, published by Kogan Page

Fairground is a simulation in which each participant keeps switching roles from that of a fairground owner who is planning a new fairground to that of a company which manufactures fairground features - rides, slides, shows, etc.

Numbers: The minimum is about six. There is no maximum.

Time: Allow about two minutes for each participant.

Materials: One copy for each participant of the FAIRGROUND PLAN and FEATURE DESCRIPTION.

Procedure: Hand out one copy to each participant of the PARTICIPANTS' NOTES and retrieve copies before the action. Hand out the FAIRGROUND PLAN and FEATURE DESCRIPTION. Arrange the room so that participants can circulate freely and have quiet corners for private discussion. Set a time limit for the completion (or partial completion) of the FEATURE DESCRIPTION.

Debriefing: Arrange for some way of publicizing the results, although this should not take long as most participants will already know what others have in their fairground. The discussion can cover the entertainments industry, publicity, promotion and sales techniques.

K. Jones 1992, published by Kogan Page

Fairground is a simulation in which each participant keeps switching roles from that of a fairground owner who is planning a new fairground to that of a company which manufactures fairground features - rides, slides, shows, etc.

You meet in pairs only, never in threes or larger groups. At the first meeting decide who takes which role, and at subsequent meetings alternate, displaying the appropriate document - either the plan for the fairground or the feature on offer - so that participants can pair up easily. There is no switching of roles during the course of a meeting, only between meetings, and you must not meet the same person twice, even if the roles are reversed.

The first stage is to decide on your feature and give it a name. It can be the usual roundabout, house of mirrors, rollercoaster, or something you have invented yourself. Write in your name and feature. Also, give a name to your own fairground and write this on your Fairground Plan. You do *not* add the feature from your manufacturer role to that of your Fairground Plan.

At the start of each meeting the pair introduce themselves, the manufacturer displays the FEATURE DESCRIPTION and the fairground owner shows the FAIRGROUND PLAN.

When an option is taken the owner writes down the manufacturer's name in an appropriate site on the plan, and no other options can be granted for that site. A fairground owner might reject a feature because it is similar to an option already acquired. Do not waste time discussing costs, safety standards and suchlike, as it is assumed that all this will be covered when the contract is drawn up.

(cut out)

....

*have pleasure in announcing a
new addition to our range of
fairground entertainments.
It is*

....

*have pleasure in announcing a
new addition to our range of
fairground entertainments.
It is*

....

*have pleasure in announcing a
new addition to our range of
fairground entertainments.
It is*

....

*have pleasure in announcing a
new addition to our range of
fairground entertainments.
It is*

....

*have pleasure in announcing a
new addition to our range of
fairground entertainments.
It is*

....

*have pleasure in announcing a
new addition to our range of
fairground entertainments.
It is*

K. Jones 1992, published by Kogan Page

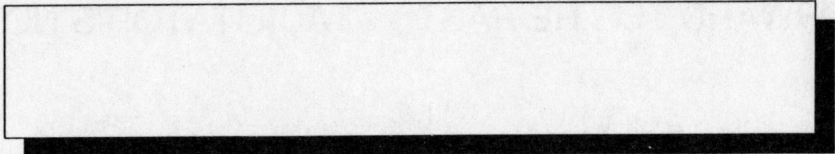

Fairground Plan

FORWARD TO THE PAST   FACILITATOR'S NOTES

Forward to the Past is a simulation in which participants are scriptwriters who have to devise a story to fit the title.

Numbers: The minimum is about six, and there is no maximum.

Time: Allow about two minutes for each participant.

Materials: One copy for each participant of the PRODUCTIONS MEMO and BRAINSTORM SHEET.

Procedure: Hand out the PARTICIPANTS' NOTES and retrieve all copies before the action begins. Hand out one copy to each participant of the PRODUCTIONS MEMO and BRAINSTORM SHEET. Provide space where the participants can mingle freely.

Debriefing: Arrange for some way of announcing the results of the session. Perhaps, more interestingly, the participants could say what ideas were rejected and why. The discussion could focus on the entertainments industry or on the advantages and disadvantages of brainstorming as a creative technique.

K. Jones 1992, published by Kogan Page

Forward to the Past is a simulation in which participants are scriptwriters who have to devise a story to fit the title.

As explained in the PRODUCTIONS MEMO meet in pairs only, and go through a fairly rapid creation of ideas. Gradually form into larger groups, depending on whether or not you are thinking along similar lines.

Write your name at the top of the BRAINSTORM SHEET and try to jot down one or two ideas on the sheet after every meeting.

Brainstorm -

and my name is ....

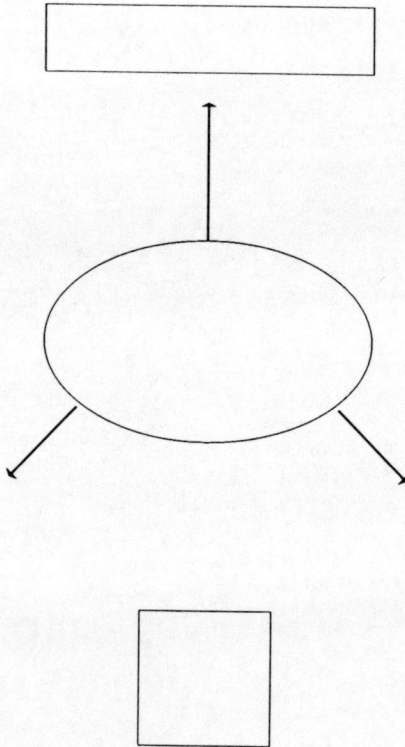

K. Jones 1992, published by Kogan Page

Productions
Memo

To: Scriptwriters

You are kindly requested to come up with some sure-fire ideas for scripts to match the ingenious and thought-provoking title put forward by our Chairman - boss of Star and Star Productions.

The title is: FORWARD TO THE PAST

How do you see it shape up - romance, comedy, tragedy, sci-fi, weepy, historical?

What could the story line be?

Don't just come up with one idea, give a million suggestions and narrow them down to a shortlist for successful hits.

The boss says 'Get them to have a corporate brainstorm' .   So do that. Put down an idea. Meet in pairs only. Write down other ideas. Join into trios. Then larger groups. Draw lines and arrows, cross out dead ends.

Organize yourselves efficiently and we are on to a winner.

LAUGH LAUGHING, INC.   FACILITATOR'S NOTES

Laugh Laughing, Inc. is a simulation about a publishing house of that name which publishes joke books and is contemplating changing its name, policy and image.

Numbers: The minimum number is about six. There is no maximum.

Time: Allow about two minutes for each participant.

Materials: One copy for each participant of the MEMO and IDEAS FORM. Clipboards could be useful.

Procedure: Hand out the PARTICIPANTS' NOTES to each participant and after a few minutes retrieve the copies before the action begins. Hand out the MEMO and IDEAS FORM. Arrange for clear space in which the participants can meet in pairs and exchange ideas.

Debriefing: Arrange for some procedure for announcing the findings. It is also worth exploring the first thoughts as well as the final outcome since the process of authorship is often more interesting than the end product. One area of discussion is managerial skills, but remember that this was an icebreaker not a test.

K. Jones 1992, published by Kogan Page

LAUGH LAUGHING, INC.   PARTICIPANTS' NOTES

Laugh Laughing, Inc. is a simulation about a publishing house of that name which publishes joke books and is contemplating changing its name, policy and image.

You are all recently appointed members of the staff of Laugh Laughing, Inc. taking part in a brainstorming session. The activity is described in the managing director's MEMO.

In the first part you just think of a few ideas - they need not be very good ideas and should not take very long. You can always develop them during the course of the simulation. The staff meet in pairs and can use the IDEAS FORM.

You are not allowed to invent specific facts about why the publishing house is not doing well. For example, you cannot say that the company produces only hardbacks, and no paperbacks. Concentrate on putting forward your own ideas and proposals. Apart from the specific facts in the MEMO just assume, as a generalization, that the company is not as efficiently run as it might be.

Laugh Laughing, Inc.

MEMO

from: MD

to: Senior Staff

When I took over this company last month I was
aware there was a major problem - falling sales.
I now realize that there are several problems
rolled into one.

1. There is over-reliance on the A JOKE A DAY
ANNUAL which still sells reasonably well,
particularly overseas, but fewer people buy it
each year and it is no longer given a prominent
position in bookshops.

2. The name of the company may not be as
suitable as it was when it was founded fifty
years ago.

3. The recently promoted 'New Jokes' series has
been a distinct flop in most areas. The best
seller in this series is 'New Jokes in Law' and
the worst is 'New Jokes in Business'.

4. The image of the Company is fuddy duddy, old
hat, a relic of a bygone era.

5. The Company's logo - 'Laughing Clown' -
might need changing.

So, have a brainstorming session. Meet in pairs
only so that you can have a brief in-depth look at
a problem. Then meet everyone in turn, but do
not form a large group. The attached form may
help.

K. Jones 1992, published by Kogan Page

Laugh Laughing, Inc.

Colleagues	Ideas	Developments

Magicians is a simulation in which members of the Magnificent Guild of Magicians are interviewed by various organizations to see if they can be offered short-term contracts. Participants alternate between the two roles of magicians and business executives.

Numbers: The minimum is about eight. There is no maximum.

Time: About ten minutes for thinking up ideas, plus about two minutes for each participant.

Materials: One copy for each pair of the NEWS HANDOUT, the MAGICIANS' CARD and the CONTRACT SHEET.

Procedure: Hand out to each participant a copy of the PARTICIPANTS' NOTES and retrieve them before the action starts. Divide the participants at random into pairs and to each pair give one copy of the NEWS HANDOUT, the MAGICIANS' CARD and the CONTRACT SHEET. Arrange the room so that the participants can circulate freely.

Debriefing: Arrange for some way of giving the details of some of the contracts. The discussion could ignore the magic and concentrate on the problems. Alternatively it could deal with the human interaction - the partnerships, creativity, analysis of problems, politeness, and effectiveness (or otherwise) of the communication skills. As mentioned on page 19 this particular simulation may generate a discussion of business ethics if the magicians object to the purpose for which the magic is intended. Despite the fantasy element, strong real-world emotions could surface. A discussion of business morality might be welcomed, but it is useful to be aware of the possibility of emotional arguments in advance of the event.

K. Jones 1992, published by Kogan Page

Magicians is a simulation in which members of the Magnificent Guild of Magicians are interviewed by various organizations to see if they can be offered short-term contracts. You alternate between the two roles - magicians and business executives.

Meet first as a pair and decide on the name and type of your organization - health farm, chocolate factory, bus company, etc - and write this on your CONTRACT SHEET. Then think of two or three (or more) situations in which magic might help your organization. You can later switch between these situational problems when you meet the different pairs of magicians. For your magician's role you just write your names on your official MAGICIANS' CARD. You could decide on a speciality in magic, but it is probably better to be a general practitioner so that you can cope with a variety of situations.

When first meeting another pair toss a coin to see which pair are the magicians and which represent the organization. At subsequent meetings alternate your positions. You do not change from being a magician to being a business executive during meetings, only between meetings.

Each meeting should be relatively brief and should start with introductions. The executives of the organization outline the situation (problem) in a few sentences. The magicians respond and either a contract is agreed or not agreed. Do not bargain or argue. Just make a fairly quick decision and move on to the next pair. If the meeting turns out to be intensely interesting and seems to be going on for more than about three minutes then someone should remark that they have another meeting to attend and the meeting should then terminate promptly.

Each meeting should be recorded by the organization executives on the CONTRACT SHEET. Choose your own way of indicating whether the contract was agreed or not. Both the magicians and the organization have the right to refuse to agree to a contract.

News Handout

Magnificent Guild of Magicians

Of late, there have been many misunderstandings, fears and false claims about magicians. We, the Magnificent Guild of Magicians, wish to clarify the position.

What we can't do

We are not gods. We cannot conjure up thunder and lightning. No blue smoke. Hard luck, chums.

What we can do

We can increase the probability of an event occurring in the future. Our best magicians can usually double the probability. For example, if the response to a company's advertisement in a trade journal is usually one reply for every thousand readers we might be able to double the probability to one reply for every 500 readers.

What we refuse to do

We do not negotiate. The rates of pay and conditions are laid down elsewhere. We accept a contract or refuse it. We do not bargain.

K. Jones 1992, published by Kogan Page

(cut out)

Magnificent Guild of Magicians

Name ....

Name ....

Magnificent Guild of Magicians

Name ....

Name ....

Magnificent Guild of Magicians

Name ....

Name ....

Magnificent Guild of Magicians

Name ....

Name ....

Contract Sheet

.... Organization

MAGICIANS	SPECIFIED JOB

K. Jones 1992, published by Kogan Page

Monolith is a simulation in which the participants are archaeologists and sociologists who have to theorize about a round stone object that has been found in a clearing in a jungle in a South American country.

Numbers: Any number from four upwards.

Time: About two minutes for each participant.

Materials: THE STONE - A REPORT, one copy for each pair.

Procedure: Divide the participants at random into pairs. Hand out one copy each of the PARTICIPANTS' NOTES and retrieve the copies before the action begins. Hand out one copy to each pair of THE STONE - A REPORT. In the first part of the action the room should have facilities for pairs to have private discussions. For the presentations, arrange a table, podium or some other focus of attention. To ensure that each pair has a chance to speak you will probably need a time limit on each presentation. You could ask for a volunteer (or two) to be timekeeper, but they must be firm in not allowing speakers to overrun their time.

Debriefing: The debriefing could discuss the theories, or the effectiveness of the presentations, or the way ancient monuments should be treated.

Monolith is a simulation in which the participants are archaeologists and sociologists who have to theorize about a large round stone object that has been found in a clearing in a jungle in a South American country.

As explained in THE STONE - A REPORT you have accepted an invitation from the National Archaeological and Sociological Association to join an expedition to inspect the stone.

Work in pairs and decide what your approach should be to the problem: how to investigate without destroying the evidence, what sort of things should be done. Put forward any theories you have about the origin and purpose of the stone.

When it is your turn to address the gathering, both members of a pair should speak. Refer to yourselves as Professor So-and-so, giving your real names. Any theories you come up with can be as speculative as you like, but must not be jokey. Your role is not that of a comic. Nor are you authors: you cannot invent facts about the stone which are not contained in the REPORT. You have not seen the stone or its location. You can speculate about it, but you must not invent 'facts' to support your speculations.

National
Archaeological and
Sociological
Association

STONE - A REPORT

Note:
Specific details of location are confidential. NASA is to organize an expedition to the site and has no desire to attract the attentions of the media, trophy hunters, or vandals.

Object: A stone, apparently man-made, completely circular, very smooth surface, with a circumference of about four metres. Our two explorers stretched their arms wide around the stone and their fingertips did not touch.

Location: Clearing in the jungle of about 100 square metres of grass and some shrubs. Stone in the centre, on a slight mound of earth. No dwellings within ten miles. No other monoliths or similar objects, although they might be overgrown in the surrounding jungle. The river is one mile away.

Theories: Our two explorers had no theories to offer. No such object has previously been reported.

Motivate is a simulation about organizations with the problem of staff who are insufficiently motivated. The participants are executives who have been asked to come up with ideas.

Numbers: The minimum is about eight. There is no maximum.

Materials: One copy for each pair of the IDEAS AND ARROWS SHEET.

Procedure: Hand out the PARTICIPANTS' NOTES to each participant and retrieve all the copies before the action starts. Divide the participants into pairs, preferably at random, and hand out the IDEAS AND ARROWS SHEET to each pair.

Debriefing: Arrange some way for pairs to announce their 'results'; this could concentrate on rejected ideas much as much as accepted ones. The discussion could look at whether motivation campaigns are useful or counter-productive, and what ways could be used to overcome problems with staff.

K. Jones 1992, published by Kogan Page

Motivate is a simulation about organizations with the problem of staff who are insufficiently motivated. The participants are executives who have been asked to come up with ideas at a conference.

You work in pairs as executives of various organizations. Before you begin, decide on your own organization - airport, furniture manufacturer, supermarket. It must be fairly large. Write this at the top of your IDEAS AND ARROWS SHEET together with your real names. Write one idea only on this sheet - and reserve the other spaces for other people's ideas.

Meet other pairs in fours, not in larger groups, and interchange one (or at the most two) ideas, showing each other your sheets. Each idea which seems viable should be written (in two or three words) on the sheet. As you collect ideas you may be able to draw arrows from one box to another to show that they are linked in some way.

Each meeting should be brief. An introduction followed by a quick exchange of one or two ideas is what is required. The ideas could be amusing, but they should be plausible. Do not make them jokey. If you cannot come up with some fairly quick responses then don't stand around in agonized thought but just say 'Thank you' and move on to the next pair.

IDEAS AND ARROWS

NAMES ....

ORGANIZATION ....

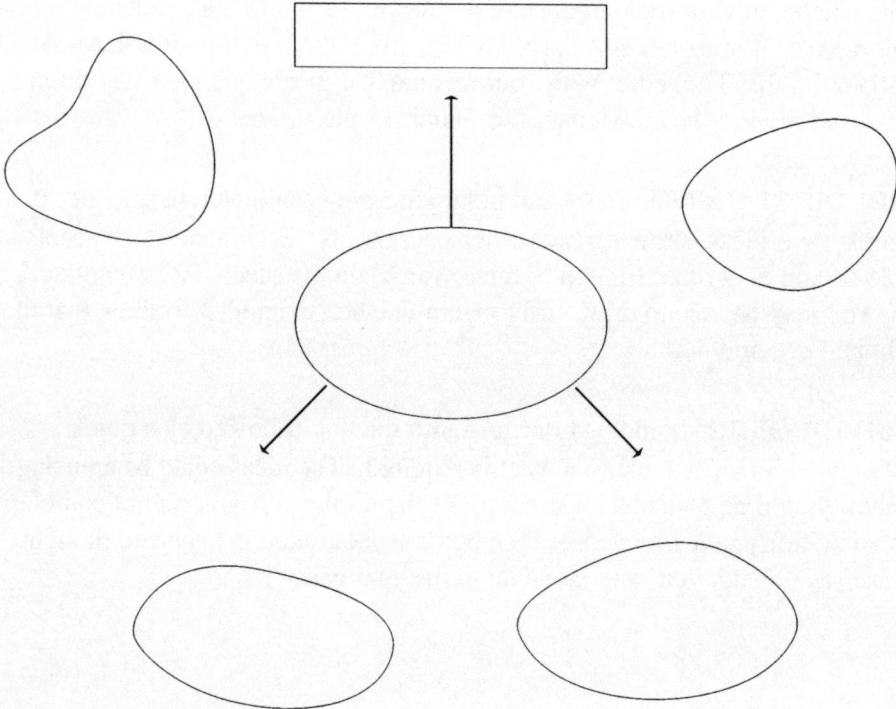

Personal Endorsements is a simulation involving surveys of the potential value of some new uses for old or used objects.

Numbers: The minimum is about eight, and there is no maximum.

Time: Allow about two minutes for each participant.

Materials: PRODUCT ASSESSMENT FORM, one copy for each pair.

Procedure: Hand out to each participant the PARTICIPANTS' NOTES and retrieve all the copies before the action starts. Divide the participants at random into pairs and give each pair a copy of the PRODUCT ASSESSMENT FORM. Clipboards would be a useful facility.

Debriefing: Make some arrangement for publicizing the findings of the surveys. If you wish to relate the simulation to the real world you could point out that turning trash into cash is big business, and in the third world is often a vital feature of the economy.

PERSONAL ENDORSEMENTS

Personal Endorsements is a simulation involving surveys of the potential value of some new uses for old or used objects.

Working in pairs, decide on a stock of old or used objects which have been received by your organization and which you wish to sell by changing their purpose. A classic example from the third world is making shoes out of used tyres. The products could be amusing - a large quantity of used toothbrushes, or a load of 'What I did on my holiday' essays from local schools. But the use to which these articles could be put should be reasonably plausible, not a joke. Aim for plausibility and invention, not 'fun'.

On the top of the PRODUCT ASSESSMENT FORM fill in the details - name, company, product and new use or adaptation. Then go round to other pairs and ask for their comments and perhaps their endorsements for the idea. At the first meeting with another pair decide who should have the role of the organization and who should be the members of the public. At subsequent meetings, alternate your roles. You should not switch roles during a meeting, only between meetings.

K. Jones 1992, published by Kogan Page

Names ....

Organization ....

Product ....

....

Details ....

....

Names	Assessment

RELATIVE LETTERS SIMULATION

Relative Letters Simulation is a simulation involving scientists seeking theories and funds regarding the relationship of certain letters.

Numbers: The minimum is probably ten, and there is no maximum.

Time: Allow about two minutes for each participant.

Materials: RESEARCH AND THEORY sheet - one copy for each pair of participants. CLUE CARDS - one sheet for every three pairs. One sheet (12 cards) of EVIDENCE CARDS for every ten participants. The reason for having more EVIDENCE CARDS than participants is that the participants can assume, if they wish to do so, that undistributed cards include letter E.

Procedure: Hand out the PARTICIPANTS' NOTES and retrieve them before the action begins. Distribute the EVIDENCE CARDS at random, placing them face down and allowing participants to pick their own. Divide the participants into pairs and give each pair a RESEARCH AND THEORY sheet. Keep the CLUE CARDS to hand out one at a time, first checking that each pair's RESEARCH AND THEORY sheet shows that the required percentage of evidence has been obtained. Arrange for a presentation area, and facilitate the presentations, including setting a time limit.

Debriefing: The words 'theory' and 'relative' are a hint that the problem might have something to do with Einstein's Theory of Relativity, which is $E=mc^2$. To find the solution before the simulation ends count the 'm' and 'c' cards remaining and deduct these two totals from the total numbers of 'm' and 'c' cards before the event began. Square the number of 'c' cards distributed to the participants and multiply it by the number of their 'm' cards. With eight participants (say 6 m and 2 c) the solution is two squared (four) multiplied by six which equals 24. If no one had heard of mc^2, or even not heard of the Theory of Relativity, it does not matter, the scientists were just pre-Einstein, and their research and theories can be judged accordingly. The discussion could begin with problem-solving ideas, including those that were rejected, and then discuss the presentations.

K. Jones 1992, published by Kogan Page

RELATIVE LETTERS SIMULATION

Relative Letters Simulation is a simulation involving scientists seeking theories and funds regarding the relationship of certain letters.

You are all scientists who collect evidence about letters. You work in pairs and meet other pairs. Each scientist has an EVIDENCE CARD containing a single letter which must be shown at all meetings. When you have discovered the letters of 20 per cent of the total number of individual participants it is assumed that you have been awarded a small research grant which has enabled you to discover a clue - so go to the Facilitator, show your list and obtain Clue Card Number One. When you have 40 per cent ask for the second clue card, 60 per cent entitles you to the third card, and 80 per cent entitles you to the fourth and last clue card. Use your RESEARCH AND THEORY sheet to formulate your ideas and classify your information. You can keep your RESEARCH AND THEORY sheet secret, or you can show it to other scientists and exchange views.

After obtaining four research grants (clue cards) you are automatically invited by a university to make a presentation of your theories and the evidence collected so far. You can accept, defer, or decline the invitation. If you make a presentation you receive no fee but you can expect applause and publicity. Both scientists in a pair should speak at their presentation and refer to each other, and any colleagues, by their real names and with the title 'Professor'. If you wish you can ask for questions from the audience after your presentation, but there will be a time limit (consult with the Facilitator).

When a presentation is being made you are an invited member of the audience. It would be impolite of you to continue to gather evidence or have private discussions while the professors were giving their presentations.

c	m	m
m	c	m
m	m	c
m	m	m

K. Jones 1992, published by Kogan Page

(Cut out)

Clue one: The answer is a number

Clue two: Alphabetic order is irrelevant

Clue three: The question is - What is the value of E?

Clue four: The answer was not known before you started

Clue one: The answer is a number

Clue two: Alphabetic order is irrelevant

Clue three: The question is - What is the value of E?

Clue four: The answer was not known before you started

Clue one: The answer is a number

Clue two: Alphabetic order is irrelevant

Clue three: The question is - What is the value of E?

Clue four: The answer was not known before you started

Worried is a simulation in which a 'worried' pair seek advice from a pair who, on request, take the roles of fortune tellers or personnel counsellors or management consultants or equal opportunity advisers.

You work together as pairs. First, fill in your names on both the RECORD OF VISIT sheet and (four times) on the FOUR-JOB CARD which can be folded according to which consultant the 'worried pair' wish to see. Now imagine that you are worried. Agree on a problem, on whether you are private individuals or an organization, and on the type of consultant you wish to see about the problem. The problem can be a 'real' problem, or imaginary, or unusual, but it should be plausible and not a joke. Note that one of the jobs is Personnel Counsellor (not Personal Counsellor) and the service deals with staff who are worried about problems at work.

At the first meeting with another pair decide who should be the consultants and which pair should be worried. At subsequent meetings change your roles. You should not switch roles during meetings, only between meetings.

The meetings should begin with the worried pair introducing themselves and asking to see one of the four types of consultants. The consultants then fold their FOUR-JOB CARD so as to reveal the appropriate section to the worried clients and introduce themselves. The meetings should be brief, lasting no more than two or three minutes at the most. If it is so interesting that it seems to be going on for longer, then someone must say that they have another meeting to attend and the discussion must end straight away.   After each meeting the consultants fill in their RECORD OF VISIT SHEET and go on to meet another pair, when they change roles to become the 'worried'.

K. Jones 1992, published by Kogan Page

(Cut out)

Fortune Tellers Name Name	**Fortune Tellers** Name Name	**Fortune Tellers** Name Name
Personnel Counsellors Name Name	**Personnel Counsellors** Name Name	**Personnel Counsellors** Name Name
Management Consultants Name Name	**Management Consultants** Name Name	**Management Consultants** Name Name
Equal Opportunities Advisers Name Name	**Equal Opportunities Advisers** Name Name	**Equal Opportunities Advisers** Name Name

Consultants' Record of Visit

Names	Problem	Advice

Zap is a simulation involving space officers and potential danger from strange creatures on the outer surface of a distant planet.

Numbers: The minimum number is about eight. It could work with seven leaving out ROLE CARD H. There is no maximum.

Time: Allow about two minutes for each participant.

Materials: One copy of the sheet containing the ROLE CARDS for each eight participants. The individual cards will need to be cut out.

Procedure: Hand out one copy of the PARTICIPANTS' NOTES to each participant (and withdraw them before the event begins). Try to arrange the room so that there is a honeycomb pattern of interconnecting paths (a classroom with rows of desks?). Allocate the ROLE CARDS at random. If there are more than eight then keep each set of cards together to avoid the danger of distributing too many of one card and too few (or none) of another card. If, say there were 20 participants then use two full sheets plus the first four cards from the next sheet.

Debriefing: The total number of heads is irrelevant. All Zaps have three arms and as there are 33 arms altogether there are 11 Zaps and they will attack. What often happens is that the participants try to find the total number of Zaps by dividing 45 by four (limbs) or five (limbs) which could mean nine, ten or eleven Zaps. However, the debriefing can concentrate not on the answer but on the strategies for arriving at it. For example, how well did the space officers communicate information and pass on suggestions for decisions?

Zap is a simulation involving space officers and potential danger from strange creatures on the outer surface of a distant planet.

You are space officers on a potentially hostile planet and have not yet had the opportunity of meeting each other properly. However, because Condition Zap has been declared on the outer surface you have been sent up from the living areas under the surface and must use the electronic pathway network which allows no more than two space officers to meet at a time. In fact, only two space officers can be on the same segment of the network at a time.

There are role cards for Space Officers A to H, each containing information about the Zaps. If there are more than eight participants and you come across someone with the identical ROLE CARD then you merge into the same space officer and must stick together.

When you meet, introduce yourselves, exchange information, and pass on your thoughts about decision-making. You can meet the same space officer more than once.

Any decision you take must be unanimous and has the status of a recommendation. You can assume that any unanimous decision is automatically relayed to Operational Control where it is likely to be approved and acted upon.

K. Jones 1992, published by Kogan Page

(cut out)

Space Officer A

Our scanners will count only the arms and heads of Zaps
A group of nine or fewer Zaps are always friendly
Some Zaps have two heads, some have one, and all have three arms

Space Officer B

All Zaps are deadly fighters and can easily kill us
A group of ten Zaps sometimes attack and sometimes are friendly
The group coming towards us has a total of 45 heads and arms

Space Officer C

A group of nine or fewer Zaps are always friendly
Each Zap has a total of either four or five arms and heads
The group coming towards us has 33 arms and 12 heads

Space Officer D

A group of ten Zaps sometimes attack and sometimes are friendly
Some Zaps have two heads, some have one, and all have three arms
Our scanners will count only the arms and heads of Zaps

Space Officer E

A group of 11 or more Zaps will always attack us
All Zaps are deadly fighters and can easily kill us
Some Zaps have two heads and some have one

Space Officer F

Each Zap has a total of either four or five arms and heads
The group coming towards us has 33 arms and 12 heads
A group of 11 or more Zaps will always attack us

Space Officer G

Some Zaps have two heads and some have one
The group coming towards us has a total of 45 heads and arms
All Zaps are deadly fighters and can easily kill us

Space Officer H

A group of nine or fewer Zaps are always friendly
A group of ten Zaps sometimes attack and sometimes are friendly
A group of 11 or more Zaps will always attack us

7

References, notes and bibliography

The account of 'sons of bitches' (page 13) is from W B G Liebrand's article 'A classification of social dilemma games' in *Simulation and Games*, 14.2 (1983). The title of this journal, which is published by SAGE, has now been changed to *Simulation and Gaming*. The other main journal in this field is the somewhat less academic, British-based *Simulation/Games for Learning*, published by Kogan Page.

My theory of ambivalents (page 14) can be found in *Interactive Learning Events: A Guide for Facilitators* which devotes a whole chapter to explanation and examples.

Icebreakers, and similar events, are free-ranging creatures which are usually corralled into subject areas such as management, communication skills, English, language teaching, games and entertainments. So if you want to see other activities which could be useful in your course then it is a good idea to glance at other corrals. It is also a good idea to look for authors and publishers as well as subjects.

Several publishers, including the one connected with this book, specialize in books about interactive learning events. The best known author is Garry Shirts, mentioned in the Acknowledgements. His STARPOWER, BAFA BAFA and WHERE DO YOU DRAW THE LINE? are eminent in the field of interactive learning events and can be obtained from McGuiver Shirts, 218 Twelfth Street, Del Mar, California. For those interested in my own works the following may be helpful, the first three being sourcebooks:

Six Simulations (1987) Basil Blackwell: Oxford and New York.
Graded Simulations (1989) Longman: London. Originally published by ILEA in 1980 under the title *Nine Graded Simulations* and by Max Hueber: Munich (1984).
A Sourcebook of Management Simulations (1989) Kogan Page: London, and Nichols: New York. This contains ten events.
Simulations in Language Teaching (1982) Cambridge University Press: Cambridge.
Designing Your Own Simulations (1985) Methuen: London.
Simulations: A Handbook for Teachers and Trainers (2nd edn. 1987) Kogan Page: London, and Nichols: New York.
Interactive Learning Events: A Guide for Facilitators (1988) Kogan Page: London, and Nichols: New York.